D1120072

Science
Experiments

CHRIS OXLADE

mustard

This edition published by Mustard, 1999
Mustard is an imprint of Parragon

Parragon
Queen Street House, 4 Queen Street
Bath, BA 1 1 HE

2 4 6 8 10 9 7 5 3

Produced by Miles Kelly Publishing Ltd,
Bardfield Centre, Great Bardfield, Essex, CM7 4SL

Printed in Spain
ISBN 1 84164 110 3

Editor: Jenny Vaughan
Project Manager: Susanne Bull
Additional editorial help from: Angela Royston
Design: Full Steam Ahead
Model photography: Mike Perry, David Lipson
Photography Ltd.
Artist: Rob Jakeway

Contents

Plants and

There are millions of different kinds of animals and plants on Earth. Each different type is called a species. They live in a huge range of habitats, from the depths of the oceans to the tops of high mountains.

Over millions of years, each species has evolved to become perfectly suited to its habitat. Some species of plants and animals have become extinct because humans have destroyed their habitats. Many species, such as tigers, are in danger because people hunt them.

This animal is a rhinoceros. It is a large mammal with a tough skin and a large horn on its snout. Rhinoceroses are becoming rare, as poachers shoot them so they can sell their horns for large sums of money.

The differences between plants and animals

Most animals can move about, and they have senses, such as sight and touch, which plants do not. Animals get the energy they need to live by eating plants or other animals. Plants live by capturing the energy in sunlight to make food.

Plants

Plants come in all sizes, from tiny single-celled algae to trees many metres high. There are several main groups of plants. Green plants include ferns and mosses, conifers and flowering plants. Flowering plants are the largest group. There are about 250,000 species of flowering plants.

Water in ponds and lakes is home to millions of tiny plants and animals, but they are too tiny to see, except through a microscope. Some of the smallest animals are made up of a single cell, just 0.5mm across.

animals

Many kinds of fungi are found on dead wood. They get the food they need from the wood. Fungi do not make seeds, as plants do. Instead, they make tiny spores that are carried away by the wind.

Fungi

Mushrooms and toadstools look like plants but they are neither plants nor animals. They are organisms called fungi. The mould which grows on rotting food is another type of fungi.

Animals

There are probably about ten million species of animal. Some, such as the blue whale, are as big as a house. Some are so small that you can only see them with a microscope. Humans belong to a group of animals called mammals. Mammals are part of a larger group of animals called vertebrates, which all have a skeleton inside their bodies. Animals without internal skeletons are called invertebrates. They include the largest group of animals – the insects.

These giant redwood trees in North America are the tallest trees in the world. They can grow over 100 metres high – twice as high as other tall fir trees. Some of them have lived for over 2000 years.

Light for growth

Plants use the energy in light to make the food they need to grow. Find out what happens if plants do not get enough light.

You will need

Cress seeds

Potting compost

A shallow tray for growing seeds

Card and scissors

3

I Fill the tray with potting compost. Sprinkle cress seeds on the surface and water them gently.

1

2 Leave the tray on a window sill, where it will get plenty of light. Check it each day to see how the seeds are growing.

3 After a few days when the leaves have formed, cut a piece of card big enough to cover the tray. Cut out a shape in the card, and put the card over the tray. Again, check it each day. What happens to the shoots under the card? How can you tell from this experiment that plants need light to grow?

Phototropism

Plants try to grow towards bright light so that their leaves get all the light they can. Scientists call this phototropism.

You will need

Cress seeds

Potting compost

Small shallow tray for seeds

Cardboard box and scissors

I Fill the tray with potting compost. Sprinkle the cress seeds on top and water them gently.

2 Cut a hole about 10cm x 10cm in the side of a cardboard box. Put the tray inside the box and put the lid on the box. Leave the box on a window sill so that light comes in through the hole.

2

WARNING!
Be careful with mould. If you touch it, wash your hands afterwards. Wash the container it was in when the experiment is over.

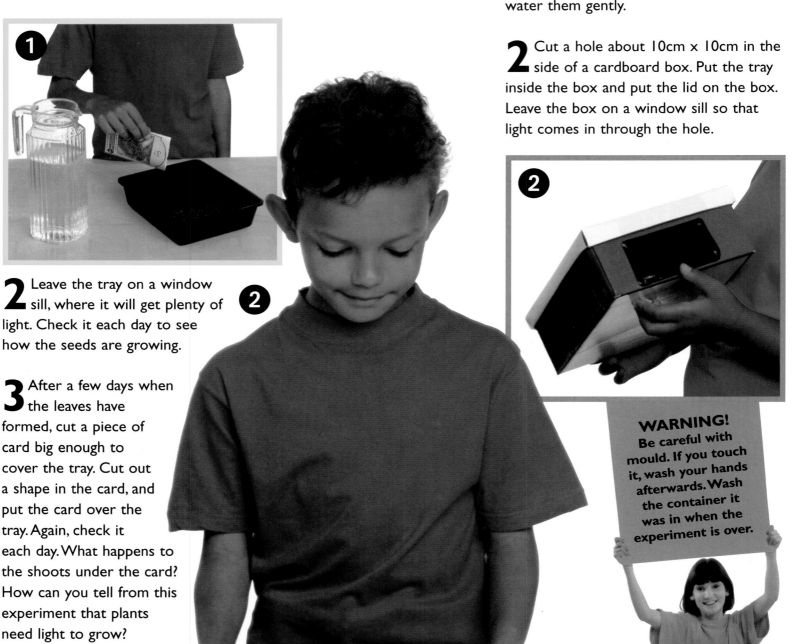

2

3 Watch the seeds as they grow. Do they grow straight upwards, or towards the hole?

❸

Ferns reproduce from spores not seeds, but they do so in a different way from moulds. First the spore grows into a small heart-shaped leaf which then develops into a fern.

Mould

Mould is a kind of fungus. You have probably seen it on old food. Try growing your own mould to study.

You will need
A small, shallow dish
Cling film, to cover the dish
Some bread
A magnifying glass

1 Put some small pieces of bread into the container. Leave it in the open air for a few hours. Add a few drops of water to the bread to make it damp. Cover the container with cling film and leave it in a warm place.

❶

❷

2 After a few days, there should be plenty of mould on the bread. Look at the mould through the cling-film. Study it with a magnifying glass. Can you see thin threads spreading across the bread, and tiny black spheres growing upwards? This type of mould is called pin mould. The black "pin heads" release minute spores that grow into more mould.

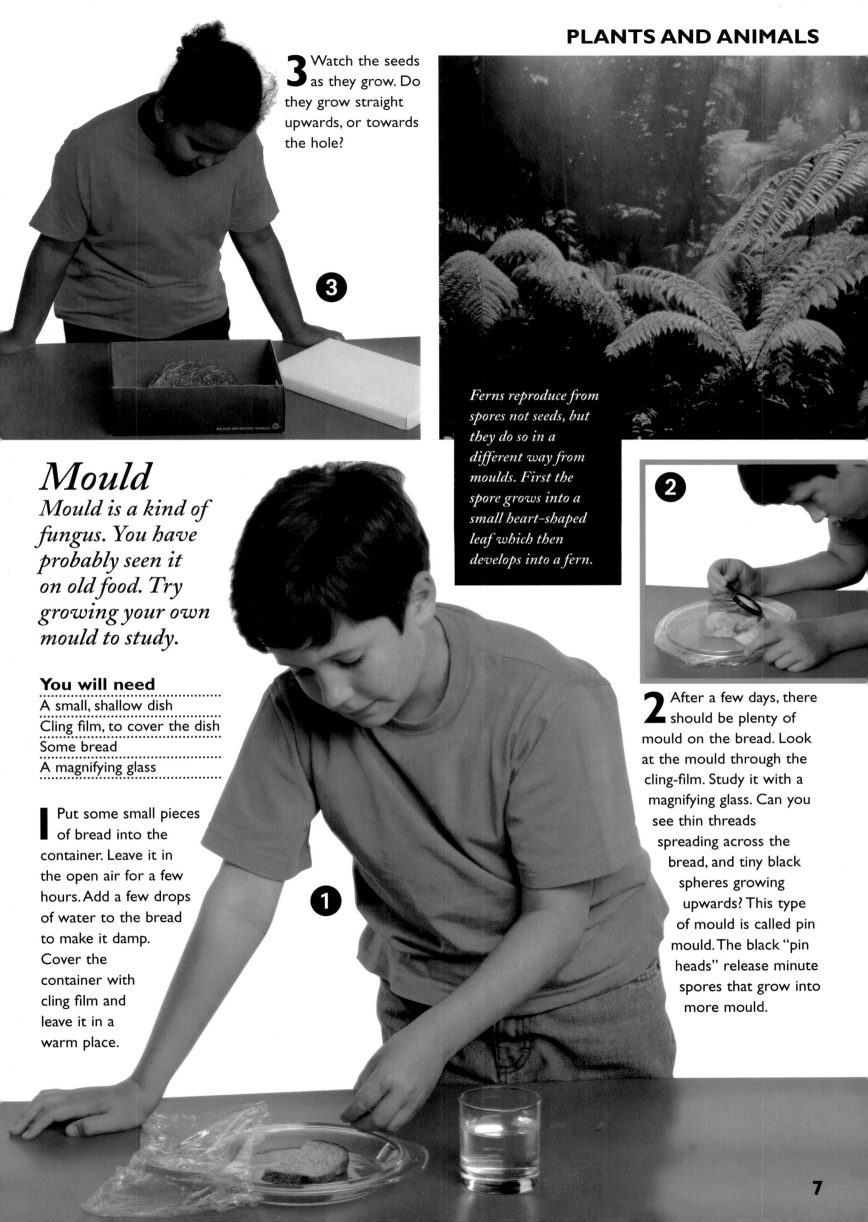

Minibeasts in the soil

The soil in your garden often has many small creatures living in it. This is how to find and study some of them.

You will need

Rubber gloves
A trowel
A jar
A sheet of plain paper
An old pencil
A magnifying glass

1 Collect a sample of soil from your garden in a jar. Choose soil that is quite loose. Spread it out on a sheet of paper. Wear your rubber gloves, and break the soil apart with the pencil, looking out for any small creatures you might see.

WARNING!
Beware of dangerous germs in soil and water. Only use soil or pond water from your garden or the school's. Always wear gloves when you work with soil or water, and wash your hands afterwards.

2 Look at the creatures with a magnifying glass. Try to make sketches of them. After you have studied them, return the creatures and soil to where you found them.

Animals in the soil do an important job. They help rot dead pieces of plant such as leaves. This turns them into nutrients that other plants need to grow. Some animals, such as worms, break up the soil and help get air into it.

Water creatures

There are tiny creatures living in streams and ponds. Have a look at a sample of water and silt to see if you can see any creatures. This is how you can do it.

You will need

Rubber gloves

Empty jars and string

A shallow glass dish

Plain white paper

A magnifying glass

A microscope

(if you have one)

I Wearing your rubber gloves, use a jar on a string to collect some water from a garden pond. If you can, collect some silt from the bottom of the pond, too. **Make sure an adult is with you when you collect the water.**

2 Take the jar home. Put the glass dish on the plain white paper and pour a little of the water into it. Now look at the water through a magnifying glass. Can you see any small creatures in it?

If you have a microscope, try using it to look at a drop of pond water.

Not all pond creatures are tiny. If you go pond-dipping, you may find a young dragonfly, or nymph. It lives under water and only leaves when it has grown wings, like the adult you can see in this picture.

Optical illusion 1

Your eyes can play tricks. We call these optical illusions.

You will need

A small ball (e.g. a golf ball)

A large ball (e.g. a football)

I Try to place the small ball in front of the large one in a way that makes them both seem to be the same size.

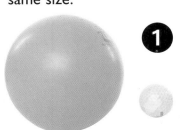

Reaction times

Most animals react when things happen to them. Try this experiment to test your own reaction time.

You will need

A ruler

A pencil and paper

I Work with a friend. Hold your hands with the palms facing each other, about 10cm apart.

2 Ask a friend to hold a ruler so that the zero on the centimetre scale is about level with the top of your palms.

3 When your friend drops the ruler, you have to catch it by clapping your hands together. Write down the position on the scale where the ruler stopped. The lower your score, the faster your reactions. Who has the fastest reaction time?

This optical illusion happens because distant objects seem smaller. If you close one eye, it makes it harder for your brain to work out distances, and you only know the large ball is further away because you also know it is larger.

Optical illusion 2

You will need

The picture at the bottom of this column

I When you stare at the cubes, do the white pieces seem to be on top of the cubes? Or do they seem to be inside them?

Like other animals, we use our eyes and brains together to judge the shape of things and their positions. Sometimes our eyes do not give our brain enough information. For example, in the picture below, it has to assume where the white pieces are, but it is not sure.

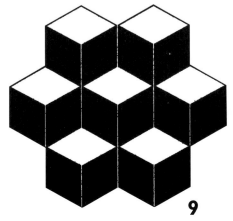

Chemistry

In chemistry, scientists called chemists investigate what substances are made of and how they behave. Chemists use their knowledge of chemistry to create new, useful substances such as plastics.

All substances are made from tiny particles called atoms. So far, scientists have discovered 109 different types of atoms. A substance made up of a single type of atom, such as oxygen, is called an element. A substance made up of different types of atom joined together is called a compound. Water is a compound of oxygen and hydrogen.

Elements

Most of the elements are shiny, grey solids when they are at room temperature. Chemists call these elements metals. They call the other elements, such as oxygen, non-metals.

Compounds

There are many thousands of different compounds. Some, such as water, are simple. Others, such as plastics, are very complicated, and contain many different elements.

Many chemicals found in animals and plants contain the element carbon. These elements are called organic compounds.

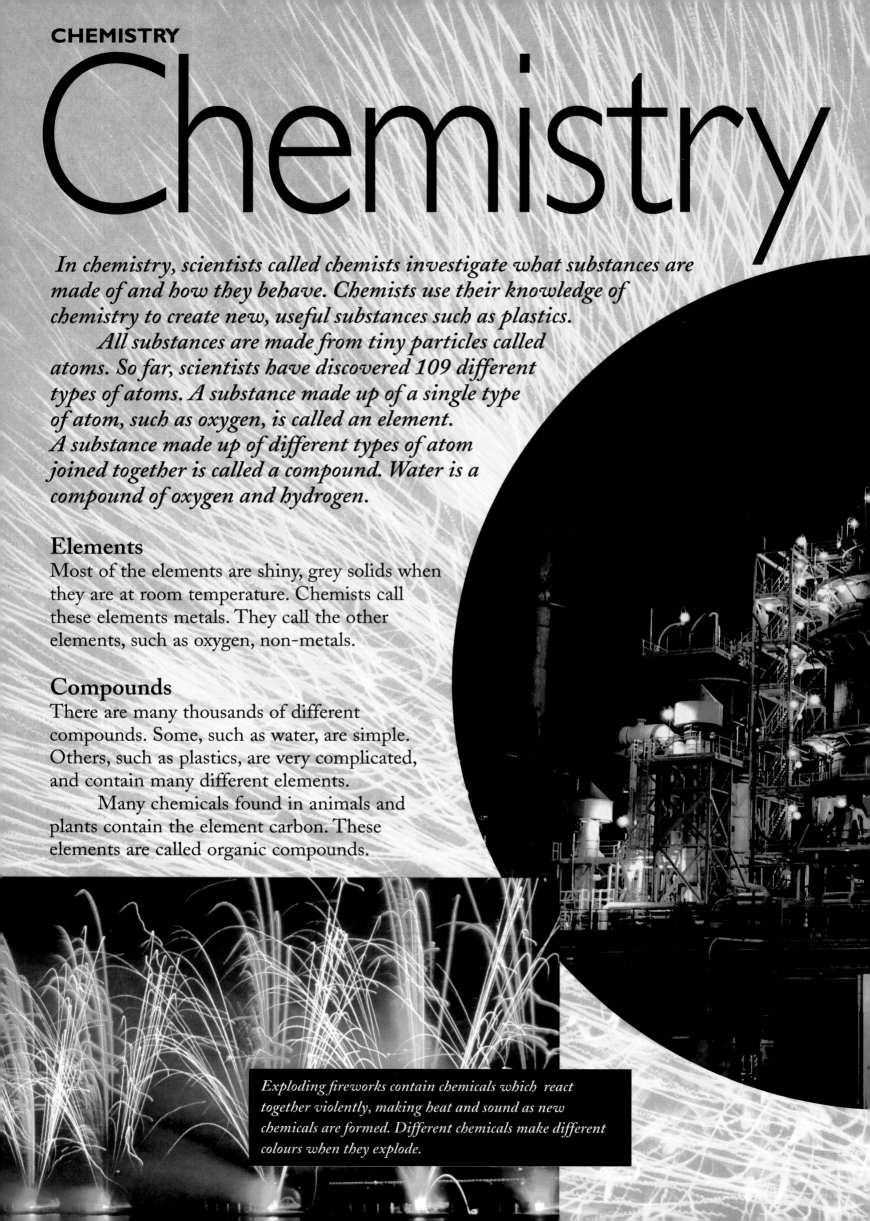

Exploding fireworks contain chemicals which react together violently, making heat and sound as new chemicals are formed. Different chemicals make different colours when they explode.

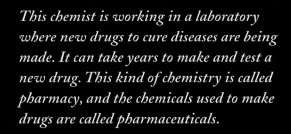

This chemist is working in a laboratory where new drugs to cure diseases are being made. It can take years to make and test a new drug. This kind of chemistry is called pharmacy, and the chemicals used to make drugs are called pharmaceuticals.

Solutions

Many substances are mixtures of different chemicals. Mixtures are different from compounds, as it is easy to separate the different substances from each other. A mixture is often in the form of a solution, where one chemical (called the solute) is dissolved in another (called the solvent). Scientists often want to find out what chemicals are in a mixture, so they try to separate the chemicals from each other. Filtering, distillation and chromatography are three different ways of separating mixtures of chemicals from each other.

Chemical reactions

Chemical reactions happen when two or more chemicals combine with each other to create new chemicals. Some chemical reactions are everyday events. These include burning, rusting, cooking and the reactions that happen in plants and animals, such as breathing and digestion. Chemists use reactions to create new chemicals.

Properties of chemicals

Materials are different from each other because they are made up of different types of atoms joined together in different amounts and different ways. This gives them their particular properties, such as their density and hardness.

Substances can be in one of three states of matter. They can be solids, liquids or gases. Most substances can change from one state to another when they are heated or cooled. In gases and liquids, the particles (atoms or groups of atoms) that make them up move about, mixing with each other. This means the liquids and gases can flow. Solids are different. The particles that make up a solid are trapped in position, and cannot flow.

Oil is a fossil fuel, formed from the remains of living things. It is made up of several organic compounds. At an oil refinery, like this one, these are separated from each other to make useful substances such as petrol.

CHEMISTRY
Diffusion

This experiment shows how two liquids mix together as the particles in them gradually mingle. This is called diffusion.

You will need

2 jars, both the same size
Petroleum jelly (e.g. Vaseline) or other grease
Food colouring
Kitchen foil
Tray

I Remove the lids from the jars and smear a layer of petroleum jelly or grease around the rim of each one.

3 Fill the other jar with tap water. Add a few drops of food colouring to it. Put it on the tray (in case of spills).

4 Carefully, turn over the jar with the foil and put it on top of the first jar.

5 Wait a few moments then, very carefully, slide out the foil.

6 Look at the jar every 15 minutes. What happens to the colour?

The tiny particles that make up the water are too small to see. But you can see how they mix together, even when you have not stirred them. You are watching diffusion taking place.

2 Fill one jar right to the brim with tap water. Put a piece of tin foil over the jar. Make sure the petroleum jelly is keeping it in place.

Making solutions

A solution forms when one substance dissolves in another. This is how to make a solution of salt or sugar and water.

You will need

Salt or sugar
Water

I Fill a jar about three-quarters full with cold water. Make a mark on the outside of the jar level with the water surface.
Add salt or sugar to the water, one level teaspoon at a time. Stir the water. Keep going until no more salt or sugar will dissolve. How many teaspoons dissolved?

2 Do the experiment again, but this time use warm water. Use the same amount of water as before. (The mark on the jar will show you how much to use.) Does more or less salt or sugar dissolve in the warmer water?

When a substance dissolves in a liquid, it breaks down into tiny particles. These mix with the particles that make up the liquid to form a solution.

Growing crystals

The particles that make up some solids are arranged neatly in rows. You can see the effect of this if you grow crystals. This is how you do it.

These amazing rocks in Northern Ireland formed millions of years ago when hot, molten rock cooled, slowly. Tall, hexagonal (six-sided) crystals were made as the rock particles formed regular patterns. The rocks are called the Giant's Causeway.

You will need

Alum powder (you can get this from a chemist)

Medium-sized jars

Cotton thread, scissors

A drinking straw

An elastic band

1 Fill a jar with warm water from a kettle. Add the alum powder a teaspoon at a time, and stir it. Allow the excess crystals to settle and carefully pour the liquid into another jar.

2 Tie a piece of cotton thread to the centre of a drinking straw. Cut the thread so that when the straw rests on the rim of the jar, it hangs down about three quarters of the way into the jar. Bend down the ends of the straw and secure them over the jar with the elastic band.

3 After a few days you should be able to see some alum crystals growing on the thread. Try to draw their shape.

alum crystals

DID YOU KNOW?
You can smell things, such as baking bread, because particles from them diffuse quickly through the air. Your nose senses the particles when you breathe the air.

Chromatography

Most inks and dyes are made up of a mixture of different pigments (substances that give them colour) in a solvent. Paper chromatography is a way of separating the different pigments from each other. This is how it's done.

You will need

Filter paper, scissors
Small canes
String
Pegs or paper clips
A shallow tray or shallow container
An elastic band
Samples of coloured liquids, for example, food colouring, pens and inks.

1 Put a large elastic band around a small tray. Push small canes through the band to make two uprights. Fill the tray with water.

2 Tie the string between the uprights. Cut strips of filter paper about 4cm wide and long enough to reach from the string into the water in the tray.

3 To test a sample, put a blob of it about 2cm from one end of a strip of filter paper. Peg the strip to the string so that only the very bottom of it hangs in the water.

4 The water will move up the paper very gradually, carrying the colours from your sample with it. You can tell from this how many colours are mixed together to make up your sample.

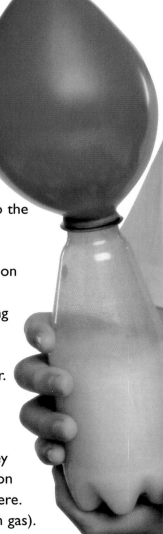

A chemical reaction

In this chemical reaction, vinegar and baking powder react together and give off a gas called carbon dioxide.

You will need

A small bottle (one that once had a fizzy drink in it)
A balloon
Vinegar
Baking powder
A funnel

1 Pour vinegar into a small bottle until it is about 1cm deep. Using a funnel, pour two teaspoons of baking powder into the neck of a balloon.

2 Stretch the neck of the balloon over the neck of the bottle, being careful not to let the baking powder out of the balloon. Now lift up the balloon so that the powder runs into the vinegar. Shake the bottle. What happens?

When two substances react together, the new substances they create are called products. Carbon dioxide is one of the products here. It inflates the balloon (fills it with gas).

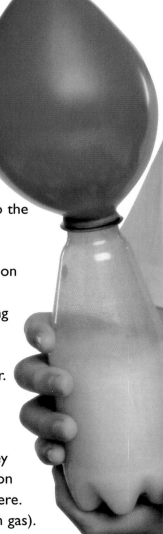

Baking powder makes cakes and buns rise. It does this because it gives off bubbles of carbon dioxide gas when it heats up. This makes the cake mixture rise. As the cake cooks the carbon dioxide bubbles are trapped in the mixture, making it spongy.

Electrolysis

Electrolysis is a way of separating the chemicals in a liquid from each other, using electricity.

You will need
Pencil leads (the sort used in propelling pencils)

A 9V battery

A length of bell wire

A compass

A jar

Some salt

1 Use a piece of bell wire about a metre long and bare the ends. Wind the middle part of the wire around a compass about 12 times.

3 Fill a jar with tap water and stir in a few teaspoons of salt. Dip the two pencil leads into the salt water and watch the compass. Does the needle twitch? That shows there is a current in the wire. Can you see gases forming on the pencil leads?

Can you smell chlorine? It comes from the salt, which is made up of chlorine and sodium. Chlorine is given off from one of the electrodes (pencil leads). The gas given off from the other electrode is hydrogen. It comes from water, which is made of the elements hydrogen and oxygen.

2 Attach one end of the wire to one terminal of the 9 volt battery and wrap the other end round a pencil lead. With another piece of wire, fix the other terminal to another pencil lead.

Air and flight

Air is a gas. We cannot see it, but we need it to breathe and stay alive. Wind is moving air and we can feel and see its effects. Air contains water vapour which sometimes forms clouds of tiny water droplets.

The atmosphere

The Earth is surrounded by a thick blanket of air called the atmosphere. It contains gases which plants and animals need to live. It also protects life from harmful rays coming from the Sun. The atmosphere gradually thins out as you go up from the Earth's surface. It eventually disappears about 650 kilometres up. The weight of the air in the atmosphere presses down from above, creating pressure called atmospheric pressure.

This huge balloon drifts through the air without the help of engines. A burner at the base of the balloon heats the air inside. The balloon becomes lighter than the air around it and rises up.

Different parts of the world have different climates. Deserts have very little rain and very hot air. Few plants can grow here. Desert nights can be very cold because dry air does not hold the heat.

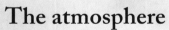

Air

Air is a mixture of different gases. It is 78 per cent nitrogen and 21 per cent oxygen. The remaining 1 per cent is made up mainly of tiny amounts of other gases, including carbon dioxide. Oxygen is needed for respiration and burning. Plants need carbon dioxide to grow.

When fuel is burned, gases that pollute the atmosphere may form. These include sulphur dioxide, which causes acid rain. Burning also produces carbon dioxide. Too much carbon dioxide in the air causes global warming.

A hurricane is a violent storm which destroys trees, crops and buildings. Winds of up to 300 km/h swirl around an area of very low pressure in the centre.

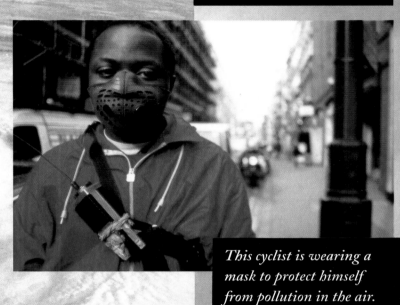

This cyclist is wearing a mask to protect himself from pollution in the air. As cars and other vehicles burn fuel, their engines emit carbon dioxide and other poisonous gases.

The weather

Heat from the Sun warms some parts of the atmosphere more than others. Hot air rises, and cooler air falls, causing the atmospheric pressure to change. This makes air move from place to place, creating winds. Water vapour in the air creates humidity and rainfall.

Using the air

Air behaves like all gases. It expands when it gets hotter and contracts when the pressure rises. Air is used in pneumatic machines to transfer movement from one place to another along pipes. Increasing the pressure at one end of the pipe makes the pressure at the other end increase too.

Flying animals and aircraft use the air to fly. To stay up, they need an upwards push called lift. Most flying things use their wings to create lift, but balloons and airships float in the air because they are very light.

Concorde is the fastest passenger plane in the world. Its pointed nose and sweptback wings reduce drag and help it to fly faster than sound. It has powerful engines, which are very noisy.

Anything that moves through air needs to overcome a force called drag. This force tries to slow things down. Flying machines use engines to overcome drag so that they can keep going. Smooth, streamlined shapes, like aircraft, make less drag.

17

What does fire do to air?

Fire needs air to burn. If you take away the air the fire goes out. Air is a mixture of gases. Find out if fire needs all the gas in the air to burn, or only part of it. Do this experiment with a candle and find out how much of the air it uses before it goes out.

You will need

A small piece of candle
Modelling clay
A shallow dish
A jar
Water

I Stand the candle in the centre of the dish. To keep it upright, you may need to hold it in place with three or four blobs of modelling clay. Make sure the top of the candle is above the level of the edge of the dish.

WARNING! Be careful when you strike the match to light the candle, and don't put your fingers too close to the candle flame. Ask an adult to help you.

2 Put three or four small blobs of clay in the dish, each one the same distance from the candle. You are going to rest the neck of the jar on these. Fill the dish with water.

3 Carefully, light the candle and then put the jar upside down over it. Balance the jar on the blobs of clay.

4 What happens? Wait until the candle goes out, then have a look at the jar. What has happened to the water that was in the dish?

Firefighters sometimes spray special foam on to a fire. This stops oxygen reaching the fire, so it can no longer burn.

Water floods into the jar, but only fills a part of it. This shows that part of the air has been used in burning, and the water has filled the space where it used to be. The part of the air that was used is the gas oxygen. It is used in breathing, as well as burning. The rest of the air that is not used in burning is made up of other gases, mostly one called nitrogen.

A weather map on television shows where there is high pressure and low pressure. High pressure normally means fine weather. Low pressure normally means that rain is on the way.

The air and the weather

Air presses down on the Earth all the time. You cannot feel it, but the pressure is always there. There is more pressure if the air is dry, and less if it is damp and rainy. We use a barometer to find out what the air pressure is. You can make your own simple barometer and use it to help you forecast the weather.

A barometer measures air pressure in millimetres and millibars (mb). Air pressure varies from place to place and can change in the space of a few hours.

1

2

3

You will need

A jar

A balloon with the neck cut off

A strong rubber band

A drinking straw

A piece of thick card

Sticky tape

Glue

A pen

1 Stretch the balloon over the top of the jar. Put the rubber band around the neck of the jar to stop the balloon slipping off.

2 Glue one end of the straw to the balloon. Use sticky tape to fix a piece of card to the jar, behind the straw. The card should be a little taller than the jar, and wide enough to reach beyond the end of the straw. Make sure it does not touch the straw.

3 Make a mark on the card to show where the end of the straw is pointing. After a few hours, mark the position of the straw again. Make a new mark every time the straw moves. Why do you think it moves? How do you think the moving straw might help you work out what the weather might be like?

DID YOU KNOW?
The Namib desert runs along the west coast of Namibia, in southern Africa. It has a very strange climate. The air is full of moisture, and there are thick fogs near the sea, but it hardly ever rains.

Hot air balloon

A hot air balloon contains air that is warmer than the air around it. Warm air is less dense than cool air (the same volume weighs less). It floats upwards – like a submerged tennis ball in water.

You will need

Tissue paper

A piece of card about 44cm long and 5cm wide

Scissors

Glue

A hairdryer

1 Cut out five squares of tissue paper and four pieces that are the other shape shown below. The diagram shows the sizes these pieces of tissue paper should be.

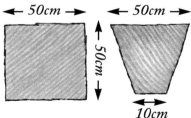

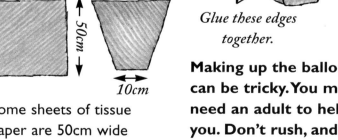

Some sheets of tissue paper are 50cm wide when you buy them.

2 Glue the pieces together. Make a cross shape, then glue together the edges of the cross.

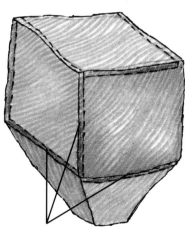

Glue these edges together.

Making up the balloon can be tricky. You may need an adult to help you. Don't rush, and don't tear the tissue.

3 Glue a card ring round the balloon's neck.

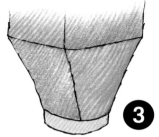

4 Point a hairdryer through the card ring and blow hot air into the tissue paper balloon. It helps if a friend holds it steady as you do this. After a while, the balloon will float upwards.

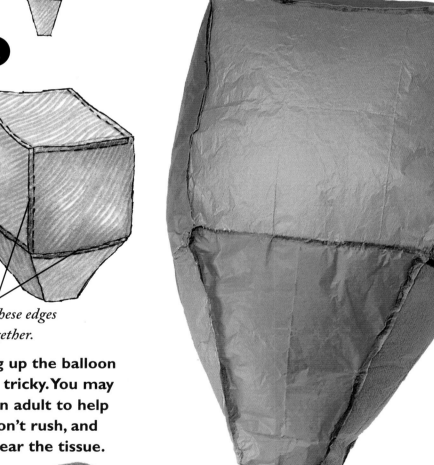

DID YOU KNOW?
Hot air balloons were invented just over 200 years ago in France by two brothers – Jacques-Étienne and Joseph-Michel Montgolfier.

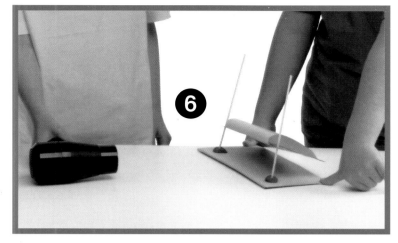

Aircraft wing

This is an experiment to show how an aircraft's wing works. The wing is an aerofoil. That means it is made in a special shape. As the wing moves, the air passing over the top of it travels faster than the air underneath it. This lifts the wing into the air.

You will need:

2 drinking straws
Modelling clay
Thin card
Stiff card
Paper
A hole punch
Scissors
Glue

1 Cut a piece of thin card 25cm x 10cm. Choose one long end to be the front and make a hole near each end. This card is your aircraft wing.

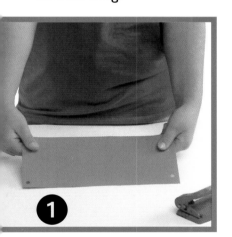

2 Cut out a baseboard about 30cm x 10cm from the stiff card. Using modelling clay, fix two straws to the baseboard so they will stick up through the holes in the wing.

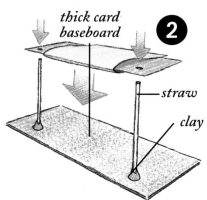

thick card baseboard
straw
clay

3 Aim a hairdryer at the wing from about 1m away. Can you get the wing to rise upwards?

As you aim the hairdryer, the base may slide back. This is because a force called drag pulls the wing backwards as air rushes over it. A flat surface like this creates a lot of drag.

4 Now make the flat wing shape into an aerofoil. To do this, start by cutting out a piece of paper almost the same size as the card wing. It must be a little shorter, and a little wider.

5 Glue the paper over the wing as the photograph shows, to make the top of it curved.

6 Aim the hairdryer at the wing again. What happens? This time, the wing lifts up more easily. Can you see how the shape of an aircraft's wing helps it to fly.

DID YOU KNOW?

The aircraft wing lifts because of the Bernoulli principle. Try the experiment at the bottom of this page to find out more about how this works.

Bernoulli's principle

Moving air creates less pressure than still air. This was discovered by Swiss scientist Daniel Bernoulli, so it is called the Bernoulli principle. Here is a simple experiment to show what it does.

You will need

Paper
A card tube
Scissors
Sticky tape

1 Cut two strips of paper about 20cm x 3cm.

Air passing between the strips exerts less pressure than the air pushing on the other side of each one. So by blowing sharply down the tube, the strips are pushed together.

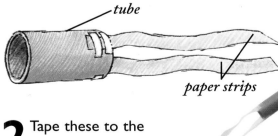

tube
paper strips

2 Tape these to the outside of a short cardboard tube.

3 Blow sharply down the tube. What happens?

Autogyro

An autogyro is a kind of aircraft that has a rotor on top. The rotor spins as air passes over it. You can see how it works by making a simple autogyro from thin card.

You will need

Thin card or stiff paper
Pencil
Ruler
Scissors
2 paper clips

1 Cut a piece of card about 40cm x 3cm. Fold it in half. Lay it flat and fold one end over 10cm from the end. Make the fold at a slight angle. The pictures show you what to do.

2 Turn the card over and fold the other end in the same way.

3 Unfold the ends to make two wings and fix two paper clips to the bottom of your autogyro.

4 Drop your autogyro from the highest place you can. The top of the stairs is a good place. Watch it spin as it falls.

Air resistance

Anything that is moving through the air has to push the air in front of it out of the way. This creates a force called air resistance, or drag, that tries to slow down the object. Some shapes let air pass around them more easily than others. These shapes keep air resistance down. Find out which shapes are best for this.

You will need

Thin card
Stiff card
Sticky tape
Scissors

1 Make three card shapes. Each one should be about 10cm high and about 4cm across. Make one a rectangle (box) shape, another a tube and the last one a fish shape.

2 Put the shapes in line on a table top. Switch on a hairdryer on a low setting. Point it at the shapes. Test them to see if they move when air is flowing towards them. Start with the dryer about a

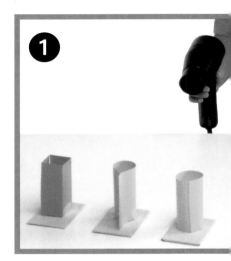

metre away. Gradually move closer. Which shape moves when the dryer is furthest away? This is the one with the most air resistance. Which shape has the least air resistance?

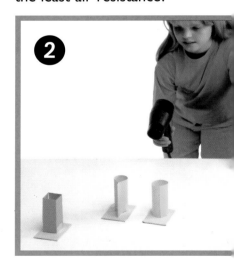

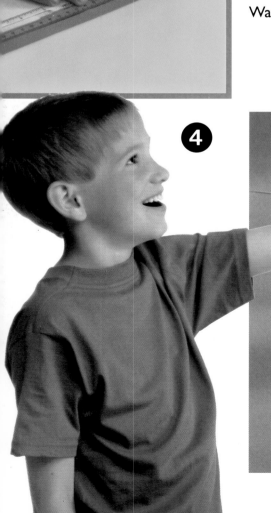

This is a real-life autogyro. It looks like a helicopter, but it works in a different way. Instead of having a motor to turn the big rotor on top, the autogyro has a propellor at the back to move it along. It is this movement that makes the rotors turn.

Wind generator

A wind generator works by using the wind to turn blades that drive a generator, to make electricity. Here is how to make blades that turn in the wind, like those of a wind generator.

You will need

A large plastic drinks bottle

A piece of thin garden cane

Round-headed map pins

A stapler

Scissors

Sticky tape

I Ask an adult to help you cut the top and bottom off the bottle to make a tube. Take care when you are cutting plastic as the edges can be sharp.

4 Put a round-headed map pin in each end of the cane. Now rest the cane on one hand or finger so that it is vertical (standing upright). Hold it gently in place with your other hand, as the picture shows. If you take your generator to a windy place and hold it in this way you will see how it spins around. It will even spin round if you blow on it.

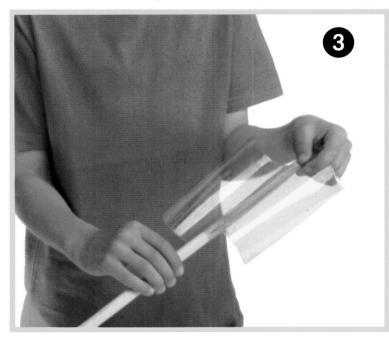

WARNING!
Cutting plastic can be difficult. You may need to ask an adult to make the first cut, with a craft knife, or safe scissors.

Cut the tube in half lengthways to make two curved vanes.

2 Overlap the edges of the vanes by 7cm or 8cm. Staple the vanes together in the corners of the overlapping area, to make the shape shown in the photographs. Leave an open slot in the middle.

3 Slide the garden cane through the slot. Tape it in place at each end.

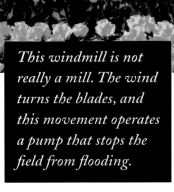

This windmill is not really a mill. The wind turns the blades, and this movement operates a pump that stops the field from flooding.

Water

Water is an unusual substance. It is a liquid at the temperatures we normally have on the Earth. Most other substances have to be heated up or cooled down before they become liquid. Oceans of water cover two-thirds of the Earth's surface, and there is water in lakes and rivers. Water is also found in the atmosphere in the form of a gas called water vapour. In very cold places, such as at the Poles and on mountain tops, it becomes solid ice.

Water and the Earth

Water is constantly evaporating from the seas into the atmosphere. It falls back down to the ground as rain, and returns to the seas along streams and rivers. Over millions of years this water has shaped the landscape by eroding the Earth's surface.

All animals and plants need water to survive. Those that live on dry land get their water from the soil or from streams, rivers and lakes. We collect and store water so we can use it for drinking, washing and irrigating crops.

A submarine usually travels deep below the surface of the water where water pressure is immense. The hull of the submarine is made of two layers of steel to withstand the pressure which acts upwards and sideways as well as downwards.

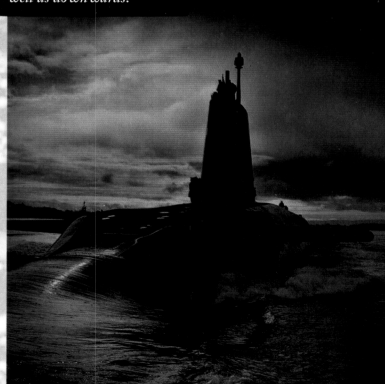

Water pressure

Underwater, the weight of the water pressing down from above creates water pressure. Water pressure makes water

The Kariba Dam in Zimbabwe is used to generate electricity. As water falls through the dam it turns huge turbines which change the energy of the water into electrical energy. About a quarter of the world's electricity is produced by hydroelectric power stations like this one.

When water freezes it forms ice. About one tenth of the oceans are covered by sheets of ice. Icebergs are parts of glaciers or ice sheets which break off and float away. They float because ice is lighter or less dense than water.

From space, the Earth looks mainly blue. This is because water covers most of its surface. Clouds float in the air. They form when water vapour in the atmosphere condenses into tiny droplets of water. This water eventually falls as rain.

flow along pipes and out of the taps in your home. Water pressure pushing up on the hull of a ship creates a force called upthrust. This pressure keeps the ship afloat and counteracts (works against) the force of gravity, which is pulling the ship downwards.

In deep water the pressure gets very high. If you dived to 100 metres, the pressure on every square centimetre of your skin would be the same as a large person standing on it. Submarines need very strong hulls so that they are not crushed by the pressure.

The surface of water

Water seems to have a stretchy elastic surface. This effect is called surface tension. It allows tiny insects to rest on the surface without falling through and it pulls small blobs of water into round drops.

Capillary action is a similar effect. It makes water flow into narrow spaces. This is what makes water flow up the narrow tubes inside the roots and stems of plants.

Scuba diving allows divers to observe the behaviour of sea creatures at close range. While under water the diver breathes oxygen stored in tanks on her back.

Vanishing water

Rain puddles gradually dry up after the rain stops. The water seems to disappear, but in fact it mixes with the air. This experiment tests whether puddles dry up faster on hot days or cold days.

You will need

Two saucers of water

Put a saucer in a warm place and pour a little water into it. Put another saucer in a cool place, with the same amount of water in it. What happens?

When water is warmed, it evaporates. It turns into a gas, water vapour, and mixes with the other gases in the air.

What happens to water when it freezes?

Most things get smaller, or contract, when they change from liquid to solid. What happens when water changes into ice?

You will need

A yoghurt pot

A saucer

A jug of water

I Fill up the yoghurt pot with water and carefully put it in the freezer.

2 Put a saucer on top of the pot and shut the freezer door. The next day, the water will be ice. Does the ice take up more or less room than the water did?

Water gets bigger and less dense as it freezes. As ice forms it comes to the surface and floats, so the water does not spill over.

Water gets bigger, or expands, when it freezes. This makes rocks crack and fall apart. These jagged mountain tops were formed by ice expanding and making the rocks break. Loose rock fell away and these sharp peaks were left behind.

Water in the air

This experiment shows that there is always water vapour in the air. You can make it condense, or change back into water.

You will need

A glass of ice-cold water

What happens to the outside of the glass of icy water? Can you see a cloudy film or drops of water on the glass? Water vapour from the air has condensed and become liquid water.

Water becomes a gas when it is warmed and may disappear into the air. It reappears as liquid when the air is cooled. The icy water cools the air around the glass, and the water vapour condenses.

④

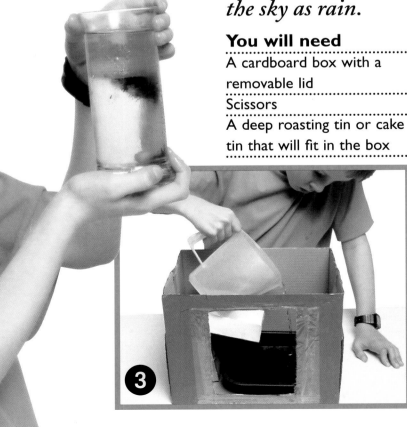

③

Make rain and a river

Make a model to show how water evaporates from the sea and falls from the sky as rain.

You will need

A cardboard box with a removable lid

Scissors

A deep roasting tin or cake tin that will fit in the box

Ice cubes

A piece of stiff card about 15cm square

A small box or other support, taller than the tray

Cling film

Sticky tape

Hot water

I Cut a hole about 10cm square at one end of the box lid. Use sticky tape to fix cling film over it. Cut a hole in the side of the box. Fix cling film over it too.

2 Put the baking tray in the box, at the other end from the hole you have cut in the lid.

3 Fold up the sides of the card to make a channel and cover it with cling film. Use the small box and sticky tape to hold it so that it slopes down towards the baking tray.

4 Fill the tray with very warm water.

5 Put the lid on the box and cover the cling film on the lid with ice. Water condenses on the cling film under the ice. This is how clouds form. It drips, like rain, into the channel and flows, like a river, into the tin – the sea.

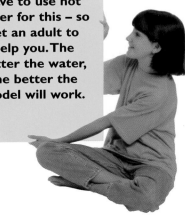

Water pressure fountain

When you are under the water, the water above presses down on you. This creates water pressure, as this experiment shows.

You will need
A plastic drinks bottle
A craft knife

1 **Ask an adult to help you cut a small hole in the bottle, using the craft knife.** It should be about 10cm from the base of the bottle.

2 Fill the bottle with water. The water escapes from the bottle as a fountain. The more water there is in the bottle, the longer the fountain gets.

The water presses downwards and forces water out through the hole. The more water there is in the bottle, the greater the pressure.

The more pressure there is, the harder the water is forced out of the hole – and the further the jet of water goes. It is a good idea to do this experiment in the bath, in a large sink or outside.

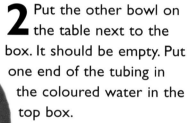

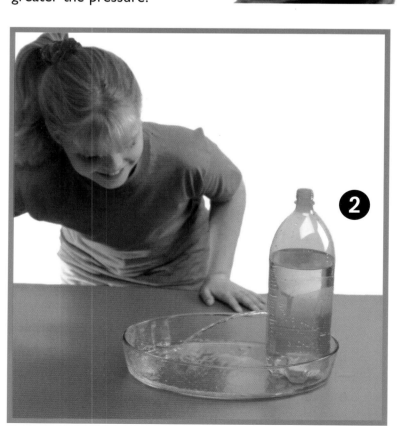

Simple siphon

How can you get water from one bowl to another, without moving either bowl? Try this experiment.

You will need
2 bowls
Some thin plastic tubing
A box
Some food colouring

1 Fill a bowl with water and put it on top of the box. Add some drops of food colouring to the water so that you will be able to see it more easily.

2 Put the other bowl on the table next to the box. It should be empty. Put one end of the tubing in the coloured water in the top box.

3 Suck the end of the tube that is not in the water. Water will travel up it to your mouth. As soon as this happens, take the end of the tube out of your mouth and put your finger over it. Put the end of the tube in the empty bowl and take your finger away. What happens?

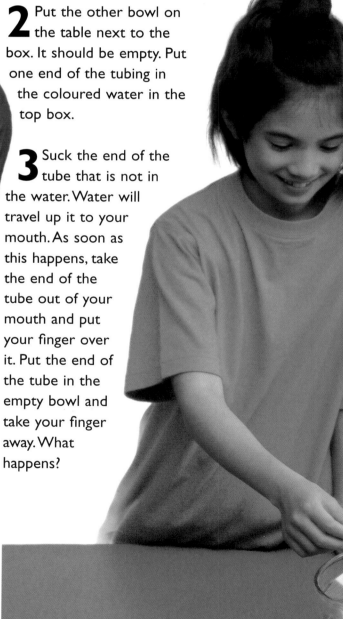

Floating and sinking

Density measures how heavy a material is. Materials, such as metal, which are more dense than water sink. Materials which are less dense than water float.

You will need

Corks

Marbles

Pieces of wood and plastic

Coins

Balls filled with air, such as table tennis balls

A bowl of water

1 Test to see how well different objects float.

Drop some small objects into a bowl of water. Light materials will float better than heavy ones.

2 Try pushing a table tennis ball under water. Can you feel the water pushing upwards? This upwards force is called 'upthrust'.

Many of these boats are made from materials that are heavier than water. They float because they are hollow. This means that, overall, they are much lighter than water. They only sink into the water a little before the upthrust from the water is enough to support them.

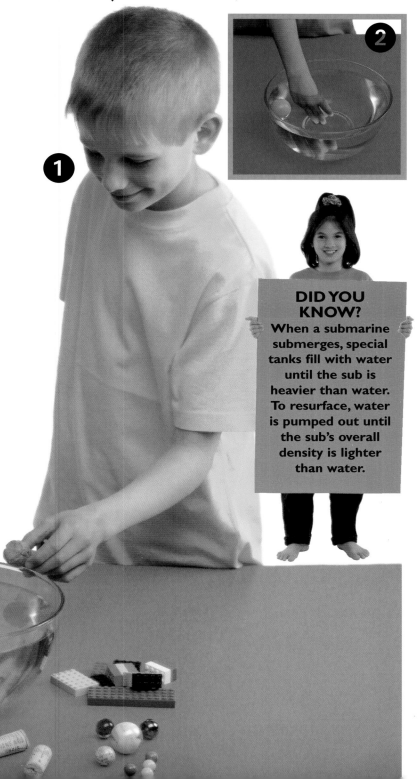

DID YOU KNOW?
When a submarine submerges, special tanks fill with water until the sub is heavier than water. To resurface, water is pumped out until the sub's overall density is lighter than water.

Model boats

Boats are heavy, but they float because they are hollow and full of air.

You will need

Bowl of water

Modelling clay

1 Put a blob of modelling clay in a bowl of water. It sinks. It is more dense than water. That means the clay weighs more than the same volume of water.

2 Now make the blob into a boat shape. Can you make it float? Upthrust from the water keeps the clay afloat.

Pond skaters can run across the pond without falling through the surface of the water. The weight of their light bodies is spread between the middle and back legs and is not enough to break the surface tension of the water.

Capillary action

Water molecules pull themselves into tiny spaces because they are attracted to other materials and also to each other.

You will need
Food colouring
Two clear plastic rulers
Blotting paper
Sticky tape, scissors
A glass of water

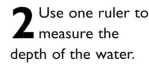

1 Fill a glass of water and add a few drops of food colouring. Look through the glass at the coloured water. Can you see how the water seems to rise up at the sides? This is called the meniscus.

2 Use one ruler to measure the depth of the water.

3 Using sticky tape, fix a strip of blotting paper to one ruler about 1cm above where the water reached. Tape the other ruler over the blotting paper, sandwiching it between the rulers.

4 Put the rulers in the water, hold them straight, so the blotting paper does not touch the water. The water should rise up between the rulers and get to the blotting paper in a few seconds.

This is called capillary action. Water molecules cling to the ruler, and to each other. They are drawn upwards between the rulers and through the tiny fibres of the blotting paper.

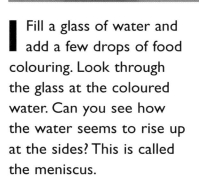

Surface tension

Water is made up of molecules which are attracted to each other. This attraction creates surface tension, which is like a stretchy skin on the surface of the water.

You will need
Some paper clips
A small bowl full of water

1 Put a paper clip on the tip of your finger and place it very carefully on top of the water. Can you get the paper clip to rest on the surface of the water and not sink?

2 Look carefully at the water around the clip. Can you see how the water surface dips down next to the paper clip?

Water wheel

Make a water turbine. In hydroelectric power stations, turbines use the energy in flowing water to generate electricity.

You will need

6 screw-on plastic bottle tops

Some bendy plastic, e.g. from a margarine tub

Waterproof glue, scissors

Stiff wire (e.g. from a coat hanger) about 30cm long

The plastic bottle you used for the fountain experiment on page 28

Two thick elastic bands or some strong sticky tape, such as insulating tape.

1 Cut two discs of plastic, both the same size, about 6cm across. Make a small hole in the middle of each one. **Ask an adult to help with this.**

3 Push the wire through the wheel and bend it as the diagram shows.

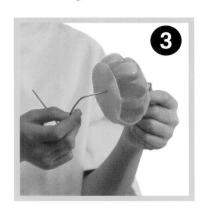

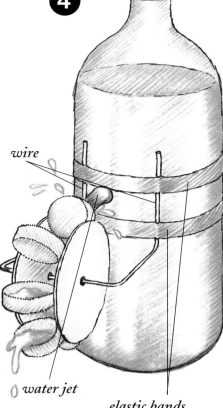

wire

water jet

elastic bands or sticky tape

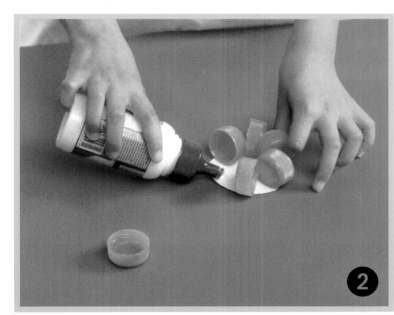

2 Glue the bottle tops around the edge of one of the discs. Fix them so that they can act as cups to catch the water as the wheel turns around. Glue the other disc over the bottle tops.

4 Fix the wheel to the bottle, using either the rubber bands or sticky tape, or both.

5 Fill the bottle with water. As water flows out of the hole, it will turn the wheel.

If you put white flowers like these in a glass of coloured water, they will slowly change colour. Plants take water into their stems through capillary action.

DID YOU KNOW?
People have captured the energy in flowing water for hundreds of years. Water wheels were used in mills to grind corn.

SOUND

Sound

Whenever something vibrates, it makes the air around it vibrate too. The vibrations spread through the air. You hear sound because your ears detect the vibrations when they get to you.

Sound waves

Vibrations travel through the air as waves of pressure. As a sound wave passes through the air, the molecules (tiny particles) of the air are stretched apart, then squashed together, pulled apart again, and so on. This makes the air pressure fall and rise.

Sound can travel through solid objects and liquids as well as through the air. In fact, it travels better through them than it does through the air.

Sound can only travel where there are particles to carry it. It cannot travel in a vacuum (an empty space). Sound cannot travel through space, because there are no particles there to carry it.

Like other waves, such as waves on water, sound bounces off solid surfaces when it hits them. An echo happens when we hear a sound once, and then hear it again because it has bounced back towards us.

In audio equipment, sound is represented by electrical signals inside the machine. Loudspeakers turn the electrical signals back into sound by vibrating the air.

A compact disc has a pattern of tiny pits on its surface. These are recorded sounds. A laser beam (a special kind of light beam) in the player reads this pattern. The player turns the pattern into sounds.

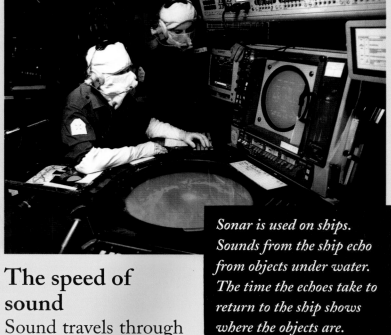

Sonar is used on ships. Sounds from the ship echo from objects under water. The time the echoes take to return to the ship shows where the objects are.

The speed of sound

Sound travels through the air at sea level at about 1,240 kilometres an hour. It travels faster in liquids and solids. Objects which travel through the air faster than the speed of sound, such as fast aircraft, are called supersonic. They create a shock wave of sound called a sonic boom.

The amplitude of a sound wave is the size of the vibrations. Sounds with larger amplitudes are louder. Their loudness is measured in decibels. The frequency of a sound is the number of vibrations which happen every second. Sounds with higher frequencies sound higher in pitch. A low sound has fewer vibrations per second.

Animals and sounds

Many animals can hear sounds with much higher or much lower pitch than humans. Many have large, sensitive ears which can detect very quiet sounds. Most animals have two ears, which allows them to work out where sounds are coming from.

Many wild animals, like these rabbits, have large ears to listen out for danger nearby. Others, such as foxes, use their large ears to listen out for prey.

Musical instruments

Musical instruments create sound in different ways. A stringed instrument, such as a violin, creates sound with a vibrating string. A wind instrument creates sound when the air inside a pipe is made to vibrate.

Percussion instruments, such as drums or xylophones, create sound when an object vibrates after it has been hit.

Spreading vibrations

Sound makes things vibrate. Do this experiment to detect the vibrations.

You will need
A balloon
A section of strong card tube (the sort used for packing posters in) about 10cm long
An elastic band
Sugar or salt
Scissors

1 Cut the neck off a balloon and stretch the balloon over one end of the tube so that it makes a tight drum.

2 Put an elastic band around the tube to keep the balloon in place.

3 Sprinkle a few grains of salt or sugar on the balloon. With your mouth about 10cm from the balloon, sing a low note. The grains should jump about. If they don't, try singing different notes. Try other kinds of noises, such as beating a drum nearby. Which sound make the grains jump the most?

Waves in a tray

Sound travels through the air in waves. This experiment shows you how waves move.

You will need
A large baking tray or other tray with high sides

1 Carefully, fill the tray with water until the surface is about 1cm from the top of the tray.

DID YOU KNOW?
Sound travels nearly four and a half times faster through water than through air. It travels more than ten times faster through wood than through air.

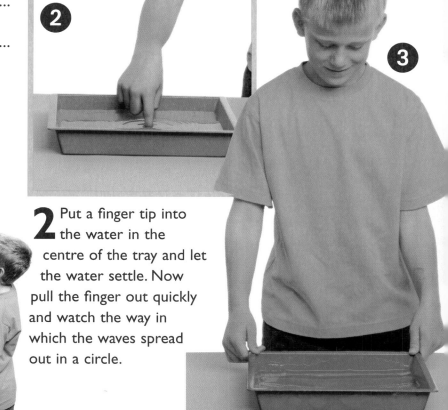

2 Put a finger tip into the water in the centre of the tray and let the water settle. Now pull the finger out quickly and watch the way in which the waves spread out in a circle.

3 Let the water settle again. When it is still, lift one end of the tray very slightly, and let it fall back quickly. Watch as a wave of water travels up and down the tray, reflecting (bouncing back) off each end.

Stereo hearing

Having two ears helps you tell where a sound is coming from. Here's a way to test this.

You will need
A blindfold
3 or 4 friends (or more)

1 Try this experiment in a large room, or out of doors. This means there will not be many echoes. Ask your friends to stand around you in a circle, about 3m away from you. Put on the blindfold.

2 Cover one ear, so that you can only hear with the other. Ask your friends to clap lightly in turn.

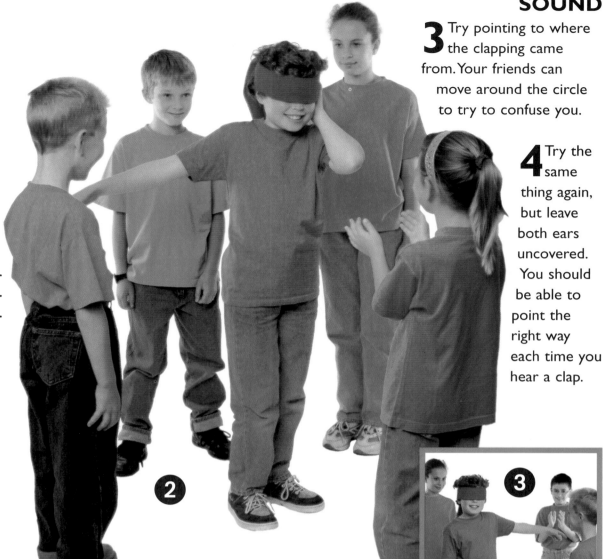

3 Try pointing to where the clapping came from. Your friends can move around the circle to try to confuse you.

4 Try the same thing again, but leave both ears uncovered. You should be able to point the right way each time you hear a clap.

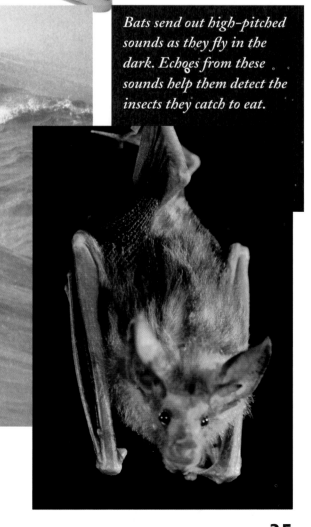

Bats send out high-pitched sounds as they fly in the dark. Echoes from these sounds help them detect the insects they catch to eat.

Waves in the sea travel along the surface of the water in an up and down movement. Sound also travels in waves, though you cannot see them. A wave is a way of carrying energy, such as sound or movement, from one place to another.

Sound from a record

Sound in an LP is recorded as a narrow groove with wavy sides. This simple record player can reproduce the sound.

You will need

Paper

Stiff card

Round-headed map pins

Drawing pins

Thick card, 40cm x 40cm

An old LP record

Scissors

Sticky tape

Glue

1 Tape a drawing pin over the hole in the middle of the LP, so the pin sticks through the hole. Stick another pin upside down, about 3cm from the centre.

drawing pins

2 Put the LP in the centre of the sheet of thick card, so it can spin on the central pin.

3 Cut a strip of stiff card 5cm x 18cm. With a map pin, pierce a hole 3cm from each end of the strip. Make the hole large enough for the pin to move in and out of it without sticking.

4 Cut a small strip of card, 5mm x 10cm. Glue it on its edge around one hole to make a ring.

5 Cut a paper disc large enough to cover the card ring. Glue the head of a map pin to its centre. When the glue is dry, glue the disc to the ring so that the pin sticks through the hole in the card strip. This is the playing needle.

6 Make a paper cone from a sheet of paper. The narrow end of the cone must fit over the card ring. Tape it in place.

7 Stick a map pin on to the sheet of thick card that the record is resting on. It should be about 2cm beyond the edge of the record, with the point sticking upwards.

card ring

8 Place the card strip so that the playing needle is on the edge of the record and the other hole in the card strip is over this pin. Use the upside-down drawing pin in the centre of the record as a handle to turn it. Listen carefully, and you will hear sounds.

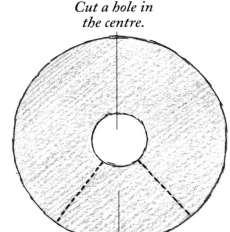

round headed map pin

paper disc

card ring

Cut a hole in the centre.

Cut this section out.

2

8

String instrument

The sounds made by a string instrument happen when the strings vibrate.

You will need

A large cardboard box

A large elastic band

Pens

Sticky tape

A craft knife

1 Using the craft knife, cut a large hole in one end of the top of the box. Ask an adult to help you.

2 Put the band over the hole and around the box. Tape a pen under it at each end of the box top.

3 Pluck the band and listen to the note. Put a thicker pen under the band, and try again. The note is higher because the part of the band that is vibrating is moving faster.

As the strings of a guitar vibrate, they make the air around them vibrate, causing a sound. The thicker strings vibrate more slowly than the thinner ones, making a deeper sound.

Wind instrument

Making air vibrate inside a tube.

You will need

At least 20 drinking straws

Stiff card

Scissors

Double-sided sticky tape

1 Cut out a piece of card about 15cm x 15cm. Stick strips of double-sided sticky tape to the card.

2 Stick 20 straws to the card, in a row. Cut across the straws at an angle, as the picture shows.

3 To play the instument, hold it near your bottom lip and blow across the top of the straws.

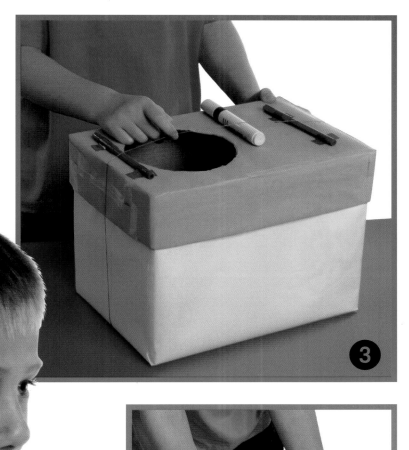

37

Light

What is light?

The light that we see every morning comes from the Sun. It is created by nuclear reactions in the Sun's centre. At night, we make light with electric light bulbs or by burning fuels. Physicists think of light as a type of wave, called an electromagnetic wave. There is a whole family of electromagnetic waves, which includes radio waves, microwaves and heat waves.

Light rays

Light travels away from its source in straight lines called rays. It travels extremely fast – around 300,000 kilometres per second.

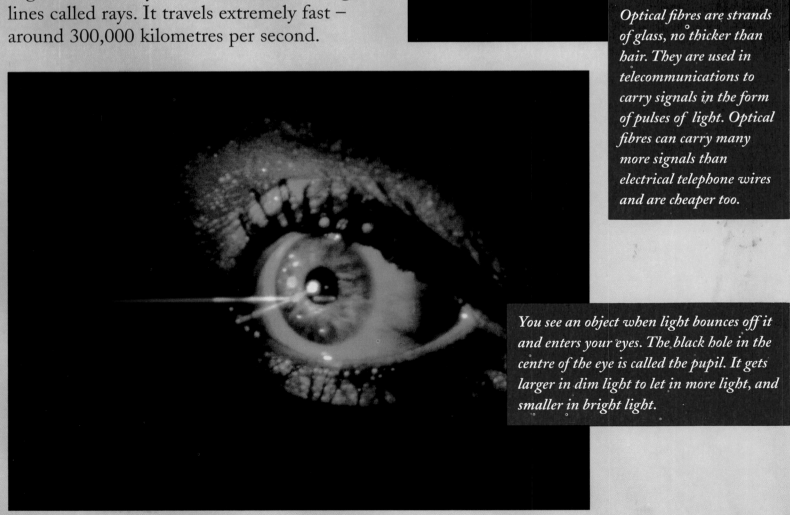

Optical fibres are strands of glass, no thicker than hair. They are used in telecommunications to carry signals in the form of pulses of light. Optical fibres can carry many more signals than electrical telephone wires and are cheaper too.

You see an object when light bounces off it and enters your eyes. The black hole in the centre of the eye is called the pupil. It gets larger in dim light to let in more light, and smaller in bright light.

Scientists think that nothing can travel faster than the speed of light. Where an object stops light rays, a patch of dark called a shadow forms on the opposite side of the object.

Reflection

When light hits a very shiny object, such as a mirror, all the light bounces off. This is called reflection. When light hits most objects, some of the light is reflected and some is absorbed. We see things because our eyes detect the light that bounces off them.

Refraction

If the object is made of something transparent, such as glass, all the light goes into it. As light passes through the boundary between two transparent materials, such as air and glass, it can change direction. This bending of light is called refraction.

Lenses, such as the ones in magnifying glasses, refract light. This makes things look larger or smaller than they really are. Curved mirrors do the same thing. Telescopes use lenses and mirrors to make distant objects look closer, while microscopes use them to make small things look larger.

Colours

The light from the Sun and light bulbs is called white light. It is made from a range of different colours of light, called the colour spectrum, mixed together. You can see the colours of the spectrum when sunlight is split up by raindrops to form a rainbow. Different colours of light can be made by mixing red, green and blue light. These are called the primary colours. All three mix together to make white.

When paints or dyes are mixed together, the primary colours are different – yellow, cyan (a shade of blue) and magenta (a shade of red). All three mix together to make black.

Many animals use colour to protect themselves from attack. These fish are brightly coloured to warn other animals that they are poisonous to eat. Others use colour to merge with their surroundings.

Sundial

Before people had clocks, they kept the time by watching the shadows made by the Sun as it moved across the sky. Here's how to make a simple shadow clock.

You will need

Some stiff card
Scissors
An atlas
A protractor
Sticky tape
A pair of compasses – for drawing circles
A compass – for finding north

1 Cut two rectangles of thick card 15cm x 30cm.

2 In an atlas, look up the latitude of where you live. The lines of latitude go across the map.

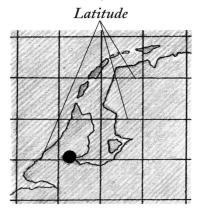

Latitude

3 Measure an angle equal to this line of latitude. Mark it on the bottom corner of one of the pieces of card. Cut along the line.

Keep this piece.

angle equal to the line of latitude

4 Draw a semi-circle on the other card, with its centre half way along one of the long edges.

5 Fix the card triangle to this base. Use small pieces of card and sticky tape to hold it in place.

6 On a sunny day, take your sundial out of doors. Using a compass, make sure the lower end of the triangle is pointing north. Then, every hour, make a mark on the card to show where the shadow of the triangle falls across the semi-circle on the base.

From now on, you can use your sundial to tell the time. Just put it outside on any sunny day, in the right position, and the shadow will show what time it is.

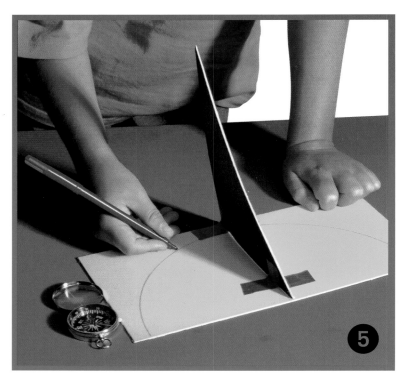

Some sundials were very beautifully made, and many people still like to own sundials, just because they look nice. Like this one, sundials often had Roman numerals. Can you work out roughly what time it is showing?

Reflecting light

This experiment shows the way that light reflects (bounces back) from a mirror.

You will need

Card
A torch
A small mirror
Scissors
Sticky putty

1 Cut a piece of card about 15cm x 10cm. Cut a narrow slot 5cm long in one edge.

2 Stand the card upright using sticky putty.

3 In a darkened room, shine a torch through the slot to make a narrow beam of light.

5 Cut two more slots in the card and try the experiment again. Can you see how the pattern of the beams stays the same on the paper as it is seen in the mirror?

4 Use the mirror to reflect the beam. Swivel the mirror from side to side to see how the direction of the beam changes.

Optical fibres

Optical fibres are transparent threads that light passes along without escaping. These fibres can carry telephone messages as flashes of light. Use a jet of water to see how they work.

You will need

A plastic drinks bottle
A craft knife
A torch

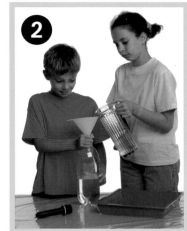

1 Cut a round hole about 5mm across, half way up a plastic drinks bottle. **Ask an adult to help you with this.**

2 Fill the bottle with water, keeping your finger over the hole. Shine a torch into the bottle, opposite the hole.

3 Move your finger and watch as the light from the torch shines along the spout of water and lights the spot where it lands.

water spout

41

How deep?

When light passes from air into water, it it is refracted (it changes direction). In this experiment, refraction makes water look less deep than it really is.

You will need

A glass tumbler

A coin

1 Put a coin in the bottom of the tumbler. Fill the tumbler with water.

2 Look down through the water. Move your finger up and down outside the tumbler until it seems to be level with the coin. Is it really level?

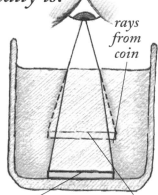

rays from coin

actual coin

rays appear to come from a coin here

In fact, the coin will seem to be less deep in the water than it really is.

Camera obscura

Try making a camera obscura – a camera with no film. It collects light from a scene and creates an image on a screen.

You will need

A small cardboard box

A magnifying glass

Tracing paper

Scissors

Sticky tape

1 First, you need to find the focal length of the lens in your magnifying glass. Hold the lens a few metres from a window. Move it around until it makes a clear image of the window on the palm of your hand. The distance between the window and the palm of your hand is the focal length of the lens of the magnifying glass.

2 Find a cardboard box that is a few centimetres longer than the focal length of the magnifying glass. Cut around the centre of the box to make two halves.

3 Cut along the edges of one side so that it slides into the other half. Fix the new edges together with sticky tape.

slits along edges

4 Cut a large hole in one end of the box and cover it with tracing paper.

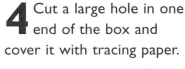

hole in end of box

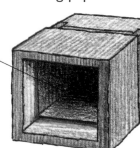

sticky taped end of box half

two halves of box – one slides into the other

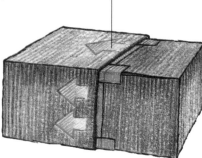

②

5 Cut a hole slightly smaller than the magnifying glass in the other end. Tape the magnifying glass over it.

6 Aim the camera at a bright object. Move the two box halves together or apart until you get a clear image of the object on the tracing paper screen.

An optical microscope uses several lenses to magnify up to 1000 times, and is used in medicine and science.

DID YOU KNOW? The image in your camera is upside down because the rays of light cross as they go through the lens.

2 Wet your finger and let a drop of water fall from it on to the hole.

3 It should form a lens shape in the hole. To use the microscope, put your eye close to the water-lens and hold an object under the lens. Move the object up and down until you can see the object clearly.

Water-drop microscope

We use lenses to help us see small objects much bigger than they really are. You can make a simple working microscope with a drop of water.

You will need

A plastic drinks bottle
A small box, such as a
    tissue box
        A hole punch
        Scissors
            Sticky tape

1 Start by cutting a narrow strip of thin plastic from a bottle or tub. It should be about 10cm x 3cm. Using a hole punch, make a hole close to one end of the strip. Next, tape the strip firmly to a small box so that the end with the hole is hanging over the edge of the box.

Making a spectrum

Light seems colourless, but it is really a mixture of colours. You can separate the colours that make up sunlight from each other. They form a rainbow of colours, which we call a spectrum.

You will need

A shallow roasting dish or small tray
White card
A small mirror
Scissors
Sticky putty

I Cut a piece of card 20cm wide x 15cm high. Cut a narrow slot in the top half of the card, as the picture shows.

2 Fill a shallow container with water.

3 Stand the container in direct sunlight. Stand the card against it, so that light shines through the slot into the water.

4 Hold the mirror at an angle in the water. Move the mirror and change the angle until a spectrum, like a rainbow, appears on the card below the slot.

When white sunlight shines through drops of rain water it breaks up and forms a spectrum.

Optical toy

An image of what we see forms on cells in our eye. These cells go on seeing the image for a short time after it has gone. This experiment shows the effect of this.

You will need

A large paper clip
Card
Tracing paper
Scissors
Glue

1 First, you will need to draw a picture. It must be in two parts. You could draw a bird and a cage, or a head with a hat. Draw your picture inside a circle about 6cm across. Cut two card circles the same size.

2 Next, trace one part of the picture on to one card circle, and the other half of the picture on to the other.

5 Hold the wire between your thumb and finger, and spin it around.

Do the two parts of your picture merge and make one picture? The image of one part of the picture lingers in your eye. As the picture twirls, this *after image* joins with the other part so that you see just one picture.

Colour filters

A colour filter lets some colours of light through, and not others. This is how to make your own colour filters, and to find out about how they work.

You will need
3 jars
Red, green and blue food colouring

1 Fill the three jars with water. Add about six drops of food colouring to each jar.

2

3 Unbend a paper clip to make a straight piece of wire.

4 Glue the two pictures together, both the same way up and facing outwards. Glue them with the wire trapped between them.

5

paper clip

6

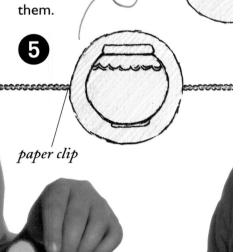

2 Hold one of the jars up to a window so that light comes through. The coloured water acts as a filter, cutting out all the colours of the light except the colour of the water. For example, red water cuts out all the colours except red, which passes through.

3 Now hold one of the jars in front of the first one you chose. Hardly any light will pass through the two jars. Can you work out why?

3

DID YOU KNOW?
Stare at a patch of bright red or green for 30 seconds and then close your eyes. You will still see a patch of colour, but it will be a different colour!

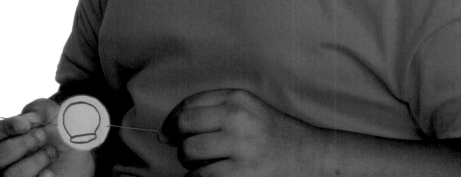

Energy and

When you feel tired, you might complain that you haven't got any energy. Energy lets you do things, such as walking to school or playing a game. But the energy in your body is not the only kind there is. In fact, nothing can happen without it.

What is energy?

Sound and light are forms of energy. Electricity is a form of energy, and so is heat. Anything that is moving has movement energy. Chemical energy is energy that is stored in chemicals such as fuels, ready to be released. It is also stored in a stretched elastic band, and in a book on a shelf. Energy can change from one form to another. When you run, you convert energy stored in your body into movement energy. Electrical energy can be changed into heat energy.

Heat energy

Heat and temperature are not the same thing. When you add heat energy to an object, its temperature rises. But a large object can contain more heat energy than a small one, although its temperature may be lower.

These wires are carrying electricity – a form of energy that can flow along wires to our homes. There, it is used to make other forms of energy, such as light.

forces

In this digger, energy from the engine makes the bucket lift and the tracks move the machine along the ground. The engine gets warm – it makes heat energy as well as movement energy.

A wind turbine is made up of blades that turn in the wind. Energy from the turbine can be used in several ways. It may work a pump, or it may be used to make electricity.

Using energy

Without energy, cars would not move along the road, household gadgets would not work, and even the weather would not happen.

At home, we use a great deal of energy every day, for heating and lighting our homes, for cooking, to work computers and televisions. Much of this energy comes to our homes in the form of electricity. Very often, electricity is made in power stations by burning fuels to release the energy in them.

Some of the energy we use is made directly by burning fuel. This is what happens with gas cookers and heaters. The energy used in cars comes from burning fuel in the engine.

Forces

A force is a push or a pull. Forces can make things start and speed up (accelerate), slow down (decelerate) and stop, change direction and spin round. They can also stretch or squash things. Some forces have special names. Friction is the force which tries to stop surfaces sliding against each other. Gravity is the force which pulls everything downwards towards the Earth.

Simple machines, such as levers and pulleys, help us to do jobs by increasing the size of the push or pull we make. For example, a light press on a pair of nutcrackers makes a very large push on the nut, making it crack.

Pressure

Pressure is the amount of force that presses on a certain area. Sharp points, such as pins, are easy to push into a surface because the force is in a small area, making high pressure. Wide tyres spread the weight of a car over a large area, making low pressure.

47

Changes of energy

Energy makes things happen. There are many different kinds of energy, and one kind can change to another. In this experiment, you can see some of the ways energy can change from one form to another – just by lifting a book and dropping it.

You will need

An old book

1 You will need an old book, because you will have to drop it, and it might get damaged.

2 Start by putting the book on the floor, then lift it slowly to shoulder height. As you do this, you are giving the book potential energy because you are lifting it up against the force of gravity, which is pulling it downwards. The energy to make it fall is there, but it is not being used. Potential means something that has not happened, but could. The energy used to raise the book is made by chemicals inside your body working together.

3 Now drop the book. The potential energy the book has gradually changes to movement energy as the book falls. Where does the energy go to when it hits the floor?

As the book hits the floor, all the potential energy you gave it has turned into movement energy. When it hits the floor, much of this energy changes to sound energy, which you hear as a bang.

Convection currents

Heat energy can travel from place to place in moving air currents. This is called convection. Here's an experiment that shows it at work.

You will need

A mug

Card

Modelling clay

A pin

Sticky tape, scissors

1 Cut a triangle of card just a little wider than the mug you are going to use in the experiment.

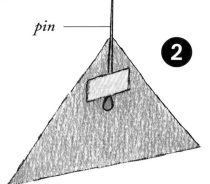

2 Tape a pin to the top corner of the card so that it points upwards.

3 Fill the mug with warm water. Rest the card triangle on the top of the mug and fix it in place with modelling clay.

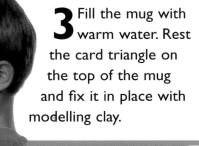

4 Cut a strip of paper 2cm x 10cm. Fold it in half at an angle to make an L shape. Open it again to make a propeller shape.

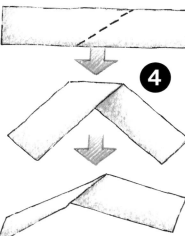

5 Balance your propeller on top of the pin and let it go. Does it begin to spin? Can you work out why this happens?

5

Look at the last experiment on this page. Can you work out why these houses on a sunny Greek island are painted white?

WARNING!
Two experiments on these pages need hot water. Ask an adult to help you. If it touches your skin, very hot water can injure you.

Radiation at work

The Sun's heat reaches the Earth by radiation. Radiation is absorbed better by dark objects than by light ones.

You will need
White card
Black card
A box, scissors

1 Cut a piece of white card and a piece of black card, both about 20cm x 20cm.

2 On a sunny day, lean both pieces of card against a box, so that the Sun's rays hit them straight on. After 5 minutes, put your hand on each card. Which feels warmer?

Heat conduction

Heat can travel through solid objects. It does this through conduction. This experiment shows that some materials are better at conducting heat than others.

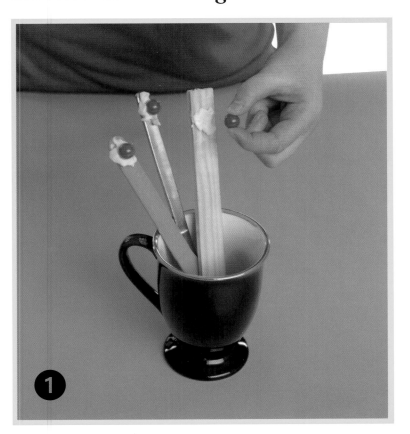

1

You will need
Metal cutlery (more than one kind of metal if this is possible)
Plastic cutlery
Strips of wood
A mug
Butter or margarine
Beads

1 Stand a few pieces of metal and plastic cutlery and the wood in a mug. Smear a blob of butter on the end of each piece and use this to stick a small bead on each blob.

2 Carefully pour hot water from a kettle into the mug. You will need an adult to help you with this. Now watch the butter and the beads. Which bead slips and falls first? What does this tell you about how well heat travels along the different materials?

The effects of forces

In this experiment, you can find out what happens when you apply different forces to an object in different places.

You will need
A large sponge

1 Put the sponge on a smooth table top. Use a finger to push it in the middle of one side. Does it move in a straight line?

2 Now push the end of one side of the sponge. What happens? With the other hand, push on the other side of the sponge. Can you make the sponge spin on the spot?

3 What happens if you press the opposite sides of the sponge? The two forces you put on it cancel each other out, but they squash the sponge.

Levers

Levers are very simple machines. We use them all the time. There are levers in scissors, pliers and many other gadgets. Here, you can see how a lever works.

You will need
A piece of wood about as wide as a ruler, about 50cm long and thicker than a ruler
Some small books
A thick pen

1 Put the pen on a flat surface and lay the wood on top of it, with the middle of the wood over the pen. The pen is now a pivot. If you apply force to one end of the wood, it will move around the pivot. The part of the wood directly over the pivot will not move up or down. The pivot on a lever is called its fulcrum.

2 Put a book on one end of the piece of the wood. Press the other end of the wood with your finger, to lift the books.

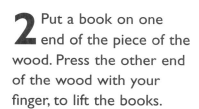

3 Now move the pen about three-quarters of the way along the wood so that it is nearer the book. Press the other end of the wood again. Do you need more or less effort to lift the book now?

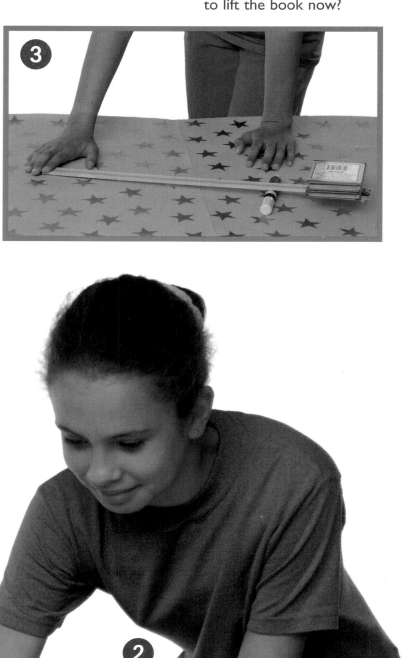

High and low pressure

The pressure a force creates depends on the area it is pressing on. Try pressing different objects into clay. The same push will exert more or less pressure on the clay, depending on the shape of the object.

You will need

Modelling clay

Some sharp and some blunt objects

I Shape a blob of the clay into a thick, flat sheet.

2 Try pressing different objects into the surface of the clay.

3 Which objects sink into it most easily?

Objects with sharp edges sink into the clay best because there is more pressure at these edges.

Each swing of the pendulum in this grandfather clock takes the same time. The pendulum keeps the clock running on time.

Pendulum swings

In this experiment, you can investigate how to make a pendulum and how to make it swing from side to side.

You will need

A piece of string at least a metre long

Some modelling clay

A stop watch

I Tie a weight, such as a blob of modelling clay, to a piece if string about a metre long. Tape the other end of the string to a support, such as a door frame, so that the weight can swing freely.

2 As this pendulum swings, gravity will pull it downwards. When it reaches the bottom of its swing and starts going up again, gravity slows it down until it stops and falls back down.

3 Swing the pendulum so that each swing is quite big. Time how long ten swings take. Then time ten smaller swings. Is there any difference between the times?

4 Add some more clay to the weight and time the swings again. Can you see why pendulums are used to control the speed of some kinds of clock?

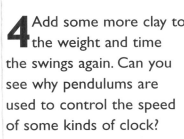

DID YOU KNOW?
Two thousand years ago, Archimedes, the Greek scientist, worked out that, if he had a long enough lever, he could lift the whole world.

Electricity magnetism

What is electricity?

Electrons and protons are two of the tiny particles which make up an atom. They are the particles that create electricity. Electricity flows when electrons move from one place to another. This happens easily in materials called conductors, that contain atoms with plenty of electrons that can move from atom to atom. Other materials have very few electrons that can move about. Electricity cannot pass through them, so they are called insulators.

Moving electrons

Rubbing two insulating materials together often makes electrons jump from one material to the other. We say the material that gains electrons gains a negative electric charge. The material which loses electrons is left with a positive electric charge. Positive and negative charges attract each other. If the charges are large enough, a spark jumps from one to the other, equalising the charges.

Electric currents

An electric current is made up of a stream of electrons in a conductor. A current can only

Officers in the navy use a compass to work out exactly where they are and which way to go. Ships have special compasses which are not affected by all the metal on the ship.

Magnets come in many shapes and sizes, but they all have two poles, called the north pole and the south pole. When two magnets are placed close to each other, the opposite poles attract each other, but the like poles repel each other.

and

These huge pylons support cables which carry electricity from the power stations, where it is generated, to towns and cities across the country.

flow when it is in a loop of conducting material called an electric circuit. There is a simple circuit inside a torch. The batteries are a store of electricity. They push the electric current through the light bulb. The current flows out of the battery, along a wire, through the light bulb, along another wire and back into the battery.

Electronics are complex electric circuits in which the flow of electricity is controlled to do a job. Computers, televisions and hi-fi systems all contain electronic circuits. Although some of these circuits are tiny, they can do complex jobs.

A computer is full of electronic circuits. These can do millions of calculations a second, create pictures on the screen, store huge amounts of information and even send information along telephone lines.

Magnets

A few materials are magnetic. That means they can be turned into a magnet. The most common magnetic material is the metal iron. All magnets have a space around them called a magnetic field where their magnetism can be felt. The field is strongest at two places on the magnet called poles.

When an electric current flows along a wire, it creates a weak magnetic field. A piece of iron with wire wrapped around it makes a strong magnet, called an electromagnet, when current flows through the wire. All electric motors contain electromagnets.

ELECTRICITY AND MAGNETISM
Conductors and insulators

Materials that electricity can pass through are called conductors. Materials it will not pass through are called insulators. This is how you find out if a material is a conductor or not.

bulb

wire

bulb holder

battery

sticky tape

wire

crocodile clips

You will need

A battery (for a torch or a radio)

Bell wire (thin, insulated wire), scissors

Sticky tape

A bulb and a bulb holder

Crocodile clips

A selection of different objects and materials to test

I Cut three pieces of wire about 50cm long. Ask an adult to help you strip the plastic covering off the ends of each piece, so that the wires are bare. Put the bulb in the bulb holder.

2 Set up a circuit like the one shown above.

3 Put different objects or materials between the crocodile clips. What happens each time?

4 If the material is a conductor, the bulb will light up. If it's an insulator, the bulb will not light up. Can you work out why?

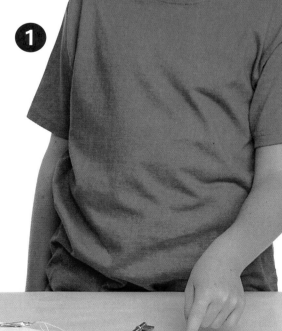

5 Try working out which sort of materials will conduct electricity (are conductors).

WARNING!
Take care! You need to use a sharp knife or the blade of a pair of scissors to cut the plastic coating away from the ends of the bell wire. Get an adult to help you.

Static electricity

Rubbing two different insulating materials together often produces opposite charges on them. This is called static electricity. Here you can see how objects charged with static electricity can pick up tiny objects, a bit like a magnet.

You will need

A plastic dustbin bag
A soft cloth
Scrap paper, scissors

1 Tear a piece of scrap paper into tiny pieces. They should be less than 5mm across. Scatter the pieces on a table.

2 Cut a piece of plastic dustbin bag about 25cm x 10cm. Lay it on the table and rub it again and

again with a cloth. This gives the plastic an electric charge, which means it has electricity on its surface.

3 Carefully lift the plastic and move it so that it is near the scraps of paper. What happens?

Forked lightning lights up the night sky. Lightning happens when static electricity jumps from a cloud to the ground. The static is made when water droplets and ice crystals hit each other inside the cloud.

Making a battery

It's quite easy to make a home-made battery.

You will need

Copper coins
Zinc nails
Kitchen foil
Crocodile clips
Bell wire (thin, insulated wire), scissors
A compass
Salt
A jar

1 Cut a piece of bell wire about a metre long. Strip off the ends of the plastic coating to leave the wires bare. Ask an adult to help you.

2 Wrap the middle part of the wire around the compass about 12 times. Connect a crocodile clip to each end of the wire.

3 Fill a jar with warm water. Stir salt into the water until no more will dissolve in it.

4 Put a copper coin on one of the crocodile clips and a piece of kitchen foil or a zinc nail on to the other one.

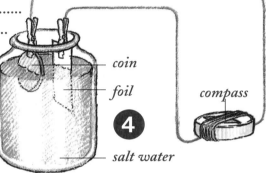

coin

foil

compass

salt water

5 Lower the clips into the salt water. Watch the compass. If the needle twitches, your battery has made an electric current that is flowing through the bell wire.

Magnetic fields

A magnetic field is the area around a magnet where it pulls iron and steel objects towards itself. The pull spreads out all around the magnet. You can draw a picture of this field, showing the direction in which the magnet is pulling.

You will need
A small compass
A selection of magnets
Sheets of paper
A pen or pencil

1 Put a magnet in the centre of a sheet of paper. Place the compass near the magnet.

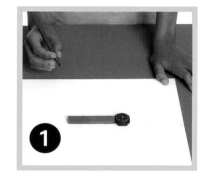

2 Draw the direction of the needle on the paper behind the compass.

3 Keep moving the compass, and drawing lines. This way you will make a picture of the magnet's magnetic field.

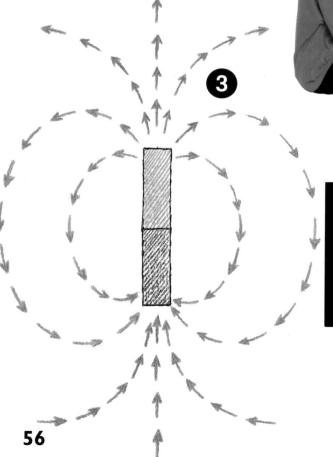

Making something magnetic

You can use a compass to make another piece of metal magnetic. Remember that you will only be able to do this with the metals iron and steel.

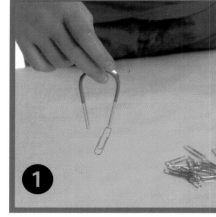

You will need
A magnet
Paper clips

1 Pick up a paper clip with a magnet. Make sure the paper clip is hanging downwards.

2 Can you pick up a second paper clip with the first? The first paper clip you picked up has been turned into a magnet itself. Scientists call this effect induced magnetism.

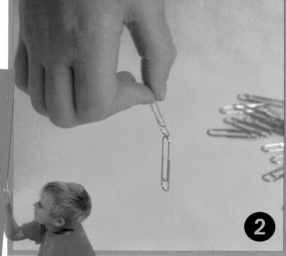

DID YOU KNOW?
The Earth itself acts like a huge magnet, and is surrounded by a magnetic field. Magnetic north is close to, but not the same as, the North Pole.

To set a compass, let the needle swing freely. Then turn the compass so that the needle lines up with north and south on the compass.

A simple compass

A compass needle is a small magnet that always points north. You can make your own compass.

You will need

A shallow dish
A cork
A craft knife
A needle
A magnet
Sticky tape

1 Use the craft knife to cut a slice, about 5mm thick, off the cork. **Ask an adult to help you.**

2 Tape the needle to the cork. Stroke the needle again and again in the same direction, with one pole (end) of a magnet.

3 Float the cork on a saucer of water. Does the needle turn to point along a north-south line?

Radio waves

Radio waves are produced whenever an electric current changes strength or direction. Make your own weak radio waves and detect them on a radio.

You will need

A medium wave radio
Bell wire (thin, insulated wire), scissors
A battery (C or D type)

1 Cut a piece of bell wire about 1m long and bare the ends. **Ask an adult to help you with this.**

2 Turn on the radio and tune it until you cannot hear a radio station and lay the wire near the radio.

3 Hold one end of the wire on one terminal of the battery and scratch the other end against the other terminal. Can you hear crackling on the radio? It is caused by the changing current in the wire creating radio waves.

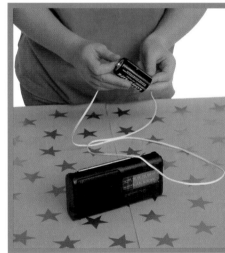

Mobile phones broadcast and receive radio waves beamed from a transmitter. Radio waves travel at the speed of light.

Making an electromagnet

You can use electricity to make a magnet that you can switch on and off.

You will need

2m bell wire (thin, insulated wire), scissors
A large steel nail or screw
Paper clips or other small metal objects
1.5 volt battery (C or D type)

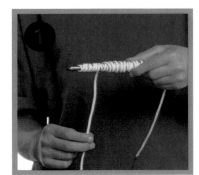

1 Strip about 2cm of insulation from both ends of 2m of bell wire, to leave bare wire. **Ask an adult to help you with this.**

2 Starting about 20cm from one end of the wire, wrap it around and around a large steel nail or screw. Work up and down until you have about 20cm of wire left.

3 Fix the ends of the wire to the two terminals of a 1.5 volt battery. Can you pick up paper clips with your electromagnet?

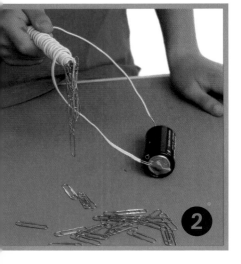

A monorail in Sydney avoids the congestion of the street below to speed people across the city. The train is driven by an electric motor.

An electric motor

You can use an electromagnet to make a motor. This is how.

You will need

Thin dowelling
Thin card
Stiff card
Paper clips
Map pins
2 1.5 volt batteries (C or D type)
2 strong bar magnets
2m bell wire (thin, insulated wire)
Kitchen foil
Scissors
Glue
Sticky tape

1 Cut a piece of stiff card about 30cm x 20cm to make a baseboard. Cut a piece of dowelling about 20cm long and push a map pin into each end, leaving about 5mm of the pin sticking out.

2 Unbend two paper clips to make supports as shown in the diagram below. Fix the paper clips to the baseboard with sticky tape so that they support the dowelling. The dowelling should be able to spin freely on its pins.

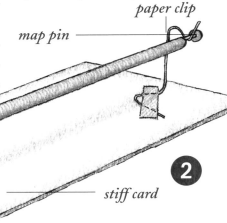

paper clip

map pin

paper clip

stiff card

3 Cut a piece of stiff card 8cm x 1cm. Fold it in half and tape it to the centre of the dowelling to make a cross shape.

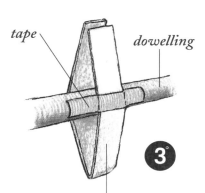

tape

dowelling

card taped to dowelling

DID YOU KNOW?
Monorails in Germany and Japan use a system called maglev. A magnetic field lifts the train above the guiding rail so that the train glides swiftly and silently along.

4

card

Keep winding the wire around the card the same way all the time.

ends of wire

4 Cut a 2m piece of bell wire and bare about 2cm of wire at both ends. Then, starting 10cm from one end of the wire, wrap it around the card until only about 10cm is left. Tape the loose ends to the dowel. This coil of wire is an important part of an electric motor. It is called an armature.

5 Cut a strip of thin card 4cm x 15cm. Tape one end of the dowelling and wrap it round and round to make a cylinder shape. Tape the end down.

6 Glue two pieces of kitchen foil to the cylinder, leaving gaps between them in line with where the armature sticks out. Tape the ends of the wire to the pieces of foil.

foil

roll of card

gap

6

another gap

DID YOU KNOW?
Electric motors are used in fans, vacuum cleaners and many household machines. They are much more efficient than petrol engines, converting 90 per cent of electrical energy into movement.

Hold wires here so one touches each piece of foil. You may have to spin the dowelling to get started.

7

magnets

7 Tape the magnets to a U-shaped piece of stiff card, with the opposite poles facing each other. Fix this to the baseboard, as the picture shows.

8 Cut two pieces of wire, each one about 30cm long. Bare about 3cm at each end. Fix the two batteries in series by taping the positive terminal of one against the negative terminal of the other. Tape the wires to the other terminals. Hold the other ends of the wires against opposite sides of the cylinder. Can you work out why the dowelling spins?

8

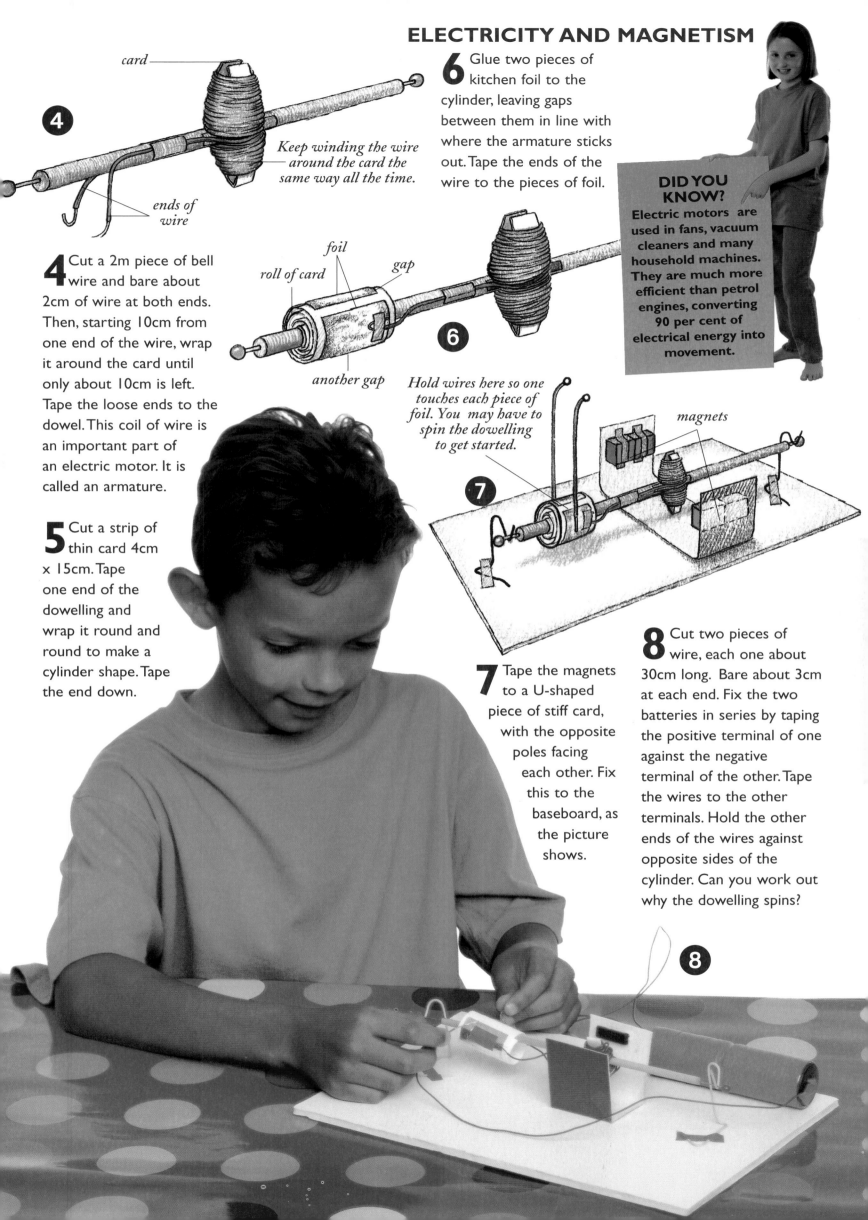

Glossary

acid rain
rain that is acidic, made when certain waste gases such as carbon dioxide react with water in the air. It can kill plants and water life, and gradually dissolve rock.

atmosphere
a blanket of air that covers the whole earth.

atmospheric pressure
the pressure is caused by the gases of the air in the atmosphere - the pressure is created by the weight of air above pressing down.

atom
the tiny particles which all substances are made of. There are more than a hundred different types of atom.

battery
a device that contains chemicals which react together to make electricity.

cell
the building blocks that animals and plants are made from. There are many different types of cell, for example, muscle cells, skin cells and nerve cells.

chromatography
a method of separating the different parts in a mixture of substances. It is used for chemical analysis.

climate
the typical pattern of weather that a place has during the year. A place with a temperate climate has warm summers and cool winters.

compound
a material that contains two or more different types of atom.

conductor
a material which allows electricity to flow through it, or a material which allows heat to flow through it well.

density
the weight of a certain amount of a substance. Steel is more dense than plastic because the same amount (volume) of steel weighs more.

distillation
a way of separating a mixture of liquids. As the mixture is heated, each part of it boils in turn, and can then be collected in the form of a gas.

electromagnet
a magnet that starts to work when an electric current is flowing through a wire.

electron
one of the very tiny particles which are part of an atom. A stream of electrons in a wire is an electric current.

element
a substance made from just one type of atom.

filter
a piece of material which contains tiny holes that trap tiny solid particles but let liquid through.

fossil
the remains of an animal or plant which have been changed into rock over millions of years.

fuel
a substance which makes a lot of heat energy when it burns.

global warming
the gradual warming of the Earth's atmosphere, caused by gases in the atmosphere trapping the Sun's heat. Scientists' think global warming may be changing the Earth's weather patterns.

gravity
the force which pulls every - thing on Earth downwards, towards the Earth's centre.

habitat
the surroundings in which an animal or plant lives.

humidity
the amount of water vapour in the air.

insulator
a material which does not let electricity flow easily through it, or a material which does not let heat flow easily through it.

irrigation
using water from streams and rivers to water crops.

latitude
the distance of a place from the equator. It is measured in degrees of angle. The latitude of the equator is 0° and the latitude of the North Pole is 90°, because the North Pole is at right angles from the equator. Lines of latitude are like imaginary horizontal lines running around the Earth from top to bottom.

lens
a piece of curved glass or plastic which bends all the rays of light coming from one point so that they meet, or appear to meet, at the same place.

longitude
the position of a place around the Earth. It is measured in degrees of angle. The Greenwich Meridian (an imaginary line running from the North to the South poles) has a longitude of 0°. The longitude of other places shows their position in relation to the Greenwich Meridian - west or east.

magnetic field
the area around a magnet where the magnet's force can be felt.

microwaves
high-energy radio waves.

molecule
a particle normally made of two or more atoms joined together. A water molecule contains one oxygen atom and two hydrogen atoms.

nuclear reaction
a reaction inside the nucleus of an atom. It happens when a nucleus splits up or when two nuclei join together.

organism
any living thing, which can be a plant, an animal or a micro-organism (such as a virus).

reflection
when a ray of light, a sound wave, or water wave, bounces off a solid surface.

refraction
when a ray of light is bent as it crosses from one material into another.

seed
the part of a plant which is scattered and can grow into a new plant.

spore
a tiny particle made by a fungus which grows into a new fungus.

water vapour
water in the form of gas. We call this change evaporation.

INDEX

Index

ACKNOWLEDGMENTS

Photographs

The publishers wish to thank the following for supplying photographs for this book:

Page 4 (BL) The Stock Market; 4 (C) MKP; 5 (TR) MKP; 5 (BR) MKP; 7 (TR) Gary Lewis/Stock Market; 8/9 (C) The Stock Market; 10 (BL) MKP; 10/11 (C) MKP; 11(TC) MKP; 11(TC) MKP; 13 (CL) MKP; 15 (TL) MKP; 16 (BL) MKP; 16 (CR) MKP; 16/17 (TC) PhotoDisc; 17 (TR) Joe Pasieka/Science Photo Library; 17 (BR) MKP; 18 (BL) Stansted Airport Ltd; 19 (BL) Justitz/ The Stock Market; 22 (BC) Mike Vines/Photolink; 23 (BR) MKP; 24(BL) British Crown Copyright/MOD. Reproduced with the permission of the Controller of Her Majesty's Stationery Office; 24/25 (TC) Mountain High CD; 24/25 (BC) MKP; 25 (TR) MKP; 25 (BR) MKP; 26 (TR) MKP; 29 (TR) MKP; 30 (TL) Claude Nuridsany and Maria Perennou; 30/31 (C) Mike Perry/David Lipson Photography; 32(BL) MKP; 32(C) 32/33 (TC) MKP; 32/33 (BC) PhotoAlto; 33 (TR) British Crown Copyright/MOD. Reproduced with the permission of the Controller of Her Majesty's Stationery Office; 35 (BL) MKP; 35 (BR) MKP; 37(TR) Susanne Bull; 38 (BL) Alexander Tsiaras/Science Photo Library; 38/39 (C) Adam Hart-Davis/Science Photo Library; 39 (BC) MKP; 40 (BR) MKP; 43 (TC) PhotoDisc; 44 (BL) MKP; 46 (BC) MKP; 46/47 (C) MKP; 47 (TR) MKP; 49 (TC) MKP; 51 (TR) MKP; 52 (CR) British Crown Copyright/MOD. Reproduced with the permission of the Controller of Her Majesty's Stationery Office; 53(CL) MKP; 53 (TR) MKP; 55(BL) MKP; 56 (BR) B. Benjamin/ The Stock Market; 57 (BR) MKP; 58(BL) MKP.

Models

Kate Birkett, Alison Cobb, Sam Connolly, Alexander Green, Jack, Robert and Sally Hutchinson, Karen Jolly, Sian Liddell, April McGhee, Alice McGhee, Nicky Maynard, Ned Miles, Aaron Phipps, Joshua Phipps, Katie Reeve, Nicholas Seels, Naomi Tayler, Chelsea Taylor.

Additional props: Vivienne Bolton and Peter Bull.

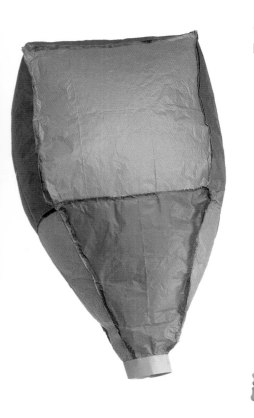